Do You Know Administration?

Attention Authors

Manas Publications is fighting a war to tell the world that India can win the battle not only by the bullet but also by pen. We are converting fighters into writers. There is no dearth of intellectuals in our country, however, their knowledge is confined to them only. No sincere effort has been made by any other publisher to channelise their knowledge, which is why the talent of every intellectual remains latent. An author always presents the raw material in the shape of a manuscript and it is the job of the publisher to convert it to a finished product. Manas has been continually motivating intellectuals and publishing their manuscripts for more than two decades and would like to publish your manuscript too. If you or your colleagues have a manuscript ready for publication or are working on it, contact us with a detailed synopsis and list of contents. Manas can also suggest you a suitable title for writing related to your area of expertise. Manas is known for its publishing quality. We take utmost care in publishing and also give wide publicity to the book and its author through our national and international distribution network.

Do You Know Administration?

Dr. Chandrika Singh
Dr. Suraj Singh Sisodiya

Manas Publications
(We Convert Fighters into Writers)
New Delhi-110002 (INDIA)

MANAS PUBLICATIONS
(Publishers, Distributors, Importers & Exporters)
4402/5-A, Ansari Road (Opp. HDFC Bank)
Darya Ganj, New Delhi-110 002 (INDIA)
Off. © 23260783, 23265523, Res. © 23842660
Fax: 011-23272766
E-mail: manaspublications@gmail.com
manaspublications@vsnl.com
Website: www.manaspublications.in

ISBN 978-81-7049-373-0
Rs. 595

Typeset at
Manas Publications

Printed in India at
RK Print Services, Delhi
and published by Mrs Suman Lata for
Manas Publications, 4402/5-A, Ansari Road
(Opp. HDFC Bank),
Darya Ganj, New Delhi-110 002 (INDIA)

Contents

Preface 7

1. Bureaucracy and Rural Development 13
2. India and Legacy of British Administrative System 38
3. Changes in Bureaucratic Framework to actualize Socio-Economic Policies 64
4. Policies and Programmes for Rural Development and Changes in Bureaucracy 92
5. Achievement and Failure of Centrally Sponsored Schemes for Rural Development 128
6. Bureaucratic Constraints in Promoting Socio-Economic Development 151

Bibliography 182

Index 198

Contents

PREFACE

Both bureaucratic administrative system and development administration are occidental concepts, which got prominence all over the world with the rise and growth of industrialization and advent of altruism. The principle of democratic altruism and increasing emphasis on establishment of egalitarian society, government is expected to be more progressive in adopting its policies and programmes keeping in view the interests of the people who are far behind in the pace of development. A government may adopt progressive policies and programmes, but desired results may not be achieved unless the bureaucrats and government officials involved in development administration take interest and work efficiently and honestly to achieve the targets. For achievement of development administration bureaucrats are expected to be more committed to implement the progressive policies and programmes of the government. Success of good governance depends upon the nature and role of bureaucracy.

participation in administration involving government servants to take active part in development administration. Due to growth of development administration the early concept of 'despotic bureaucracy' is fast changing to 'committed bureaucracy.' Currently, the roles of bureaucrats are not only concerned with maintenance of law and order and collection of revenues, but also related to people's welfare. Keeping in view stagnant economy of India due to long colonial rule and economic backwardness of the people, the government of India applied all the possible efforts to gear up country's economy and help people in their self-development by introducing development administration and decentralizing the power to enable the local authorities to make development administration a success.

In Weberian formulation bureaucracy is characterized as 'values-neutral theory', which means the bureaucrats are recruited through an independent as well as neutral agency (Public Service Commission) on the basis of merits. As the permanent government servants, they must refrain from party politics. In the words of Peter Blau bureaucracy should be considered as "an organization that maximizes efficiency in administration or an institutionalized method of organized social conduct in the interest of administrative efficiency." The bureaucrats are selected officials of the government who are generally trained and work under strict discipline on the hierarchal line of control. Whether the society is capitalist or socialist, reality is that bureaucracy is an indispensable force.

Development administration as a concept is as new as the concept of welfare state. The root of development administration may be found in the concept of good governance, which puts emphasis on welfare state ensuring conditions of good life to all. Like public administration, development administration is also amorphous combination of theory and practice. Development is a growth into "a better, fuller, higher and mature condition" It is an aspect of change that is desirable broadly predicted and planned or at least influenced by governmental action." Development administration has further been defined as "state of mind, a tendency, a direction, rather than a fixed goal. It is a rate of change in particular direction".

Development administration has four basic objectives i.e policy making, planning, programmes and projects.

Presently, development administration has assumed both macro and micro approaches of development. The issues related to it are poverty alleviation, institutional development at local, district, state and national level, good governance, environmental protection, structural development etc.

India inherited from the British a monolithic and strictly hierarchical administrative structure, which required certain modifications keeping in view the constitutional objectives of the nation. The constitution of India grants its people economic and political, equality of status, of opportunity and before law making India a welfare state. To achieve these objectives the need was felt to make the Indian bureaucratic system more result-oriented. The organizational principles and the structural-functional base of the Indian bureaucratic system remained as it were during the British rule in India, but changes were made in the purpose, nature and responsibility of the bureaucratic system. The Constitution incorporated provisions to provide special protection to the services of the Indian bureaucrats and administrators so that they may work independently and efficiently. The All India Service Amendment Act 1963 created some more All India Services. The scope of authority and responsibility of the bureaucrats increased to a great extent with the launching of more development schemes and projects under various Five Year Plans. Time came when bureaucracy in India came down to the level of districts and development blocks to help the rural agencies to implement numerous development programmes in the rural fields.

Development administration in India began with the formation of the first Congress government under the leadership of Pt. Jawaharlal Nehru, who believed in sicialism but he was yet not ready to take dynamic steps to work for socialistic pattern of society.

However, his government constituted the Planning Commission, the National Development Council, the Committee on Plan projects, Research Programme Committee etc. with the marked objective to gear up Indian economy. To help the farmers the government also launched the Community Development Project in 1952 covering the whole nation. The basic lapse of the CDP was that, it had no programme for the people of deprived and suppressed sections. Moreover, due to supremacy of bureaucrats the CDP could hardly achieve the desired goal. The CDP became a 'bureaucratically guided programme' where bureaucrats played vital role in formulating and implementing programmes.

Development administration in India got real pace during the regime of Mrs. Indira Gandhi and Rajiv Gandhi. She directed the planners to make a shift in planning from macro-level to micro-level. Under such shift, preference was given to the people living below the line of poverty first time in India. Thereafter, the Integrated Rural Development Programme (IRDP) covering all aspects of rural life all over the country was launched in 1980 during the Sixth Five Year Plan (1973–83), which further opened new dimensions in the field of development administration. It was a package programme of various rural development services and activities of government. It was a nationwide movement which aimed at eradicating poverty from the rural areas by providing jobs to the majority of rural poor and other facilities for their all round development providing them easy loans along with sufficient subsidies. It also aimed to change the rural face by providing the people village approach roads and linking the villages with the main roads.

With the passage of years, the policies and programmes related to development administration especially for the rural areas went on multiplying one after another. The Sixth and Seventh Five Year Plans put much emphasis on rural development under the IRDP which consisted of various centrally sponsored development programmes such as TRYSEM, NREP, and RLEP etc. Very recently

National Rural Employment Guarantee Programme (NREGP) was introduced with the purpose to provide employment to the rural poor at least 100 days in a year with guarantee. Thus, it is obvious that the government of India paid due attention towards development of rural India. This has increased the overall responsibility of the government and its officials for the welfare of the people.

It was expected that both the government and its officials would help people to get rid of perpetual poverty, but poverty is still a dominant ugly feature of the country. The results of the development administration achieved so far are not encouraging due to emerging damaging trends, which have badly affected the growth of development administration in India. Bureaucrats are largely responsible for it because they tend to become handmaiden of the politicians who use them for their personsl benefits. The corrupt high officials are not in a position to control over their subordinates because of the fear of being exposed. Continuous decline in moral standard in public life, which has become the regular feature of India, is the serious factor responsible for corrupt practices. Various scams which are coming to notice amply prove that both the ministers and bureaucrats keeping aside their morality, are single-mindedly engaged in money-making at the cost of the nation and its people. Another trend which has harmed the development administration is politicization of administration which has become a tool of administrators to act as middlemen of the ministers.

These trends which have recently emerged in the Indian administrative system have affected the growth of development administration needing a thorough study and examination. The present work describes the conceptual meaning of bureaucracy and development administration and analyses the role of bureaucrats towards development administration. It also investigates into the causes of slow progress in the field of development. It examines in details the factors involved in development administration, which have recently emerged and are responsible for sinking the country into mass corruption.

Finally, we acknowledge all those officials and authorities who enabled us to complete the work by sharing the views and opinions with us regarding development administration and rural development in India. Thanks to the libertarians and their staff of various public and private libraries for their kind cooperation in collection of related materials. It is expected that this book will prove useful to the scholars and the crusaders against the corruption.

Chandrika Singh

Suraj Singh Sisodiya

Chapter – I

Bureaucracy and Rural Development

In the fast changing and developing world of today, administration is playing notable role. The remotest corners of a nation are being developed. To make administration more effective and enable maximum people participation in the process of developmental administration, various changes have been made in the organizational pattern of administrative structure. Today, development is the first priority everywhere. The question arises: what is development?

Development is a change from old to new, from traditional to modern and from backwardness to forwardness. Development is an effort to change the human society for better future. At the end of the day people's or a nation's will to move towards progress and prosperity where there is no scarcity of essential needs, to say the least. Again, development is a march towards building a new nation self-sufficient and self-dependent. As a sequel local self-government has been assigned with various development-related tasks commensurate with the area and its inhabitants. Local Self-Government is an integral part of a political system, meant to broaden the scope of people's participation in self-governance. The need of a democratic society based on the principles of equality and liberty has been to create maximum avenues of development to enable its citizens to derive maximum benefits from the development plans and programmes of the government, with special attention to the development of rural India where nearly 80 per cent people live. Substantial part of this 80 per cent populace lives below the poverty line (BPL). Under the process of development administration, the Government of India has made effective changes in the rural governing institutions as well as bureaucratic system. The Village Panchayat plays a vital role in the implementation of development schemes and programmes launched by the government from time to time. In that way the local self-government has become a link between the government and the people of the peripheries thereby enabling them to work for self-development. Besides, the government has effected several changes in the organizational pattern of bureaucracy on the one hand, and decentralized the power on the other to enable the local governing institutions to work effectively.

Bureaucracy is generally understood as an epithet for 'inefficiency and red tape'. The concept of bureaucracy is related to understanding the organization of modern society, government and business. It is an integral part of the Government. No government can handle its affairs without the set of appointed officials who are committed and responsible for implementing the policies and programmes of the government. Bureaucracy is the modern nomenclature of the officers who managed the State affairs in the medieval period or for that matter even in the ancient times. However, in the present epoch of democracy and industrialization, the government has effected several changes in the administrative machinery to meet the needs of the day. Presently, bureaucracy has become dimensional in its approach and multifarious in actions. The structure of civil society, during ancient period, was simple. Hence, the administrative machinery of the government was not complicated. Advent of industrialization and also democratic socialism made bureaucratic system more and more responsive and responsible. With the growth of parliamentary democracy based on party system, emphasis on neutralism of bureaucracy was felt. Moreover, concept of welfare state, which paved the way for the growth of development administration enlarged the scope of bureaucracy on the one hand, and involved people in participation of administration for their self development on the other. Emerging awareness among the people and their growing political consciousness has made them active participants in various welfare schemes and programmes of the government. Again, attention of the government towards people's problems and commitment to improve the lot of the deprived and suppressed sections of the people has further increased the role and significance of bureaucracy. Thus, all these factors have not only expanded the scope of bureaucracy but also made it more responsible to the populace as a whole. There was the time when the character of bureaucracy was despotic. The bureaucrats were responsible mostly for maintenance of law and order and collection of revenues. It was the democratic and socialistic principles, gaining their ascendancy in the social framework, which paved the way for the growth of development administration. As a result, the scope of administration has increased and the government officials from top to bottom have been involved in development administration assuming duties and responsibilities to implement the development policies and programmes of the government for the general well-being of people. Thus, with the rise and growth of development administration the significance and role of bureaucracy have increased making it more complex and technical in structure and more elastic in approach and behaviour.

Conceptual Framework of Bureaucracy

According to the *Concise Oxford English Dictionary* bureaucracy means a "system of government in which most decisions are taken by state officials rather than by elected representatives"[1]. A bureaucrat is a government official who endeavours to concentrate administrative power in his bureau. He is a member of bureaucracy.[2] As stated above, the term bureaucracy is a modern concept rooted in the idea of Max Weber and Morstein Marx who have given scientific meaning to bureaucracy. According to Max Weber, bureaucratic model is usually placed in the category of classical administrative thought and the Weberian 'ideal type.' The term bureaucracy was first used in the French form as *BUREAUCRATIE* in the eighteenth century. In the nineteenth century, it spread in Germany as *BIRBOKRATIE*. Thereafter, it reached England and from there it traveled to other parts of the world.[3] It was Karl Marx, Max Weber and Robert Michaels who enlarged the term and presented clear concept of bureaucracy. According to Marx, bureaucracy like the state itself is an instrument by which the dominant class exercises its domination over social classes which are not in a position to repulse the weight of the dominant classes. According to this logic, the interests of the bureaucracy are closely linked to those who rule and administer the state keeping their values safe and secured. Explaining more about bureaucracy, Marx says that it is a form of society dominated by the state and its tendency is to separate itself from the content. It assumes 'formalism' and as such presents itself as a superior 'consciousness' as the will of the state.[4] Thus the Marxist line of thinking about bureaucracy is related to the class conflicts and quite contrary to the views of the western liberal thinkers about bureaucracy. Marx viewed bureaucracy as a viable tool in the hands of the ruling class with the marked purpose to plan and implement the programmes for development and protection of the ruling as well as affluent class on the one hand and to suppress the rivals on the other. Since the bureaucrats are chosen by the government supported by the rich, they are legally and morally bound to work for their interest. Since the existence and maintenance of the bureaucrats, according to the Marxist view, totally depend upon the rich, they can never act against the interest of their masters.

Bureaucracy in Western View: Max Weber's Idea

The idea of Karl Marx about concept of bureaucracy was never acceptable to those who supported western view of liberalism because the former pleaded for class war and replacement of a new society based on principles of socialism. Hence, the political philosophers and thinkers who believed in philosophy of liberalism and democratic socialism developed new concept of bureaucracy. In western countries, especially in the United States, the idea and meaning of bureaucracy is more inclined towards the orthodox Weberian line. The American idea of bureaucracy has been mechanical and conservative. Again, the western bureaucratic idea is largely based on capitalistic pattern of society. Since modern term of bureaucracy is mostly related to Max Weber's idea, it would be better to have a cursory glance over the Weberian concept of bureaucracy. Max Weber, while searching the origin of bureaucracy, found its genesis in whole of the Roman Empire. He observed that weak Roman Empire could not maintain law and order and failed to control the officials who had not only dominated the ruler but also connived for monetary benefits and better living standard. They imposed heavy taxation to objectives. To quote Max Weber, "The development of the money economy is a presupposition of bureaucracy." Increasing needs for public revenue compels the state to develop a rational system or public finance. To quote Weber once again, "a stable system of taxation is the precondition for the permanent existence of bureaucratic administration."[5] Stable economies can be given by stable administration. Max Weber further stated that a second prerequisite of bureaucratic growth was the demand of the larger middle class for the benefit of mass democracy, especially for social and economic equality. Bureaucratic development, as Weber observed, was closely associated with the negation of the practice of special privileges. "Bureaucracy", according to Max Weber, "inevitably accompanies modern mass democracy. This the characteristic principle of bureaucracy; the abstract regularity of the execution of authority, which is a result of the demand for equality before the law and the principled rejection of doing business."[6] Weberian formulation of bureaucracy has been characterized as values-neutral theory. It simply provides a conceptualization of a form of social organization with certain characteristics. It can be examined from three different points of view, which are not, exclusive: First bureaucracy can be viewed in terms of purely structural characteristic. In fact, the structural dimension has attracted the most attention in the discussion on bureaucracy. The features like division of work and hierarchy have been identified as important aspects of structure. Second, bureaucracy has been sought to be defined in terms of behavioural characteristics. Certain patterns of behaviour form an integral part of conception. Said Weber, "When fully developed, bureaucracy also stands in a specific sense under the principle of superiority its specific nature, which is welcomed by capitalism, develops when democracy becomes more complicated, and it also becomes more 'dehumanized'. This is the specific nature of bureaucracy and it is its specific nature where business supersedes humanism".[7] Third, bureaucracy has been looked at from the point of view of achievement of purposes. This is an instrumental view of bureaucracy. As Peter Blau suggests, it should be considered as "an organization that maximizes efficiency in administration or an institutionalized method of organized social conduct in the interest of administrative efficiency."[8]

Weber's concept of bureaucracy is rooted in the growth of business management, which appeared with the rise of industrialization. Weber's writing on bureaucracy and rationalization of modern life is the seminal text that underpins virtually all subsequent theory and writing about business. Weber sees business as central to comprehending modern society. His theory seems as a keystone to subsequent consideration of business. Gauldner, too, supports the Weberian view of bureaucracy, and tests his theory within industrial setting. According to him the consideration of bureaucracy relied on documentary evidence.[9] Peter Blau also presents theoretical premise and considers bureaucratic authority related to business and democracy. Blau is aware of the fact that bureaucracy in modern fast changing milieu of social change has to play a vital role to uphold the required changes and maintain balance between different social groups and agents. Rourke finds role and significance of bureaucratic organization related to public policy. To him bureaucracy is increasingly the focus of investigation into 'policy failures', When policy goals are not achieved, the obvious scapegoat is the organization (bureaucracy) charged with their attachment.[10]

New meaning and concept of bureaucracy provided it stable and honourable place in the system of administration across the world. A need was felt not to disturb bureaucrats and to provide them independent status devoid of political interference so that they could work independently and efficiently. In a democratic country, the ruling party changes when the opinion of the electorate changes about its ability and viability to rule over the people. But the bureaucrats who are chosen people and those who remain neutral run the administration. Thus, it is obvious that bureaucratic system has recent development and it got strength first in the western countries. It is such a system, which consists of chosen officials who are generally trained and work under strict discipline. Their services are recorded. Most of the democratic states have provided bureaucrats constitutional status and they cannot be punished or charged until they violate provisions made for protection of their services. The officials employed in bureaucratic structure of administration have the order of command on the pyramidical basis. The most important feature of bureaucracy is that it stands collectively to achieve prescribed goals. With the development of democratic model of administration bureaucrats are expected to act neutrally. They are known as permanent executives not supposed to involve in party politics or take interest in politics. The government of a political party is the subject of change, but bureaucrats remain in service till the date of their superannuation. Again, with increasing attention of the government towards the principles of socialistic pattern of society, the nature and role of bureaucracy is changing by the day on the one hand, and its responsibility to participate in development administration on the other.

The expectation from modern bureaucracy is to take more interest in implementing welfare schemes of the government for the people and share greater responsibility in removing poverty from the state. Max Weber has rightly remarked that the development of modern form of the organization of corporate group in all fields is nothing less than identical with the development and continual spirit of bureaucratic administration. In his own words, "Its development is to take the most striking case; the most crucial phenomenon ...the whole pattern of everyday life is to cut to fit the framework of administration."[11] Growing political consciousnesses of people and their active participation in party politics have changed the nature of politics today. No party may gain majority or remain in power for long until their policies and programmes are related to the policy of welfare and well-being of the masses. To implement such policies and programmes there is a need for permanent well-trained officials having needed skills and commitments. This has not only increased the role and responsibility of bureaucrats but also made their position more significant.

Bureaucracy and Civil Service

In Weberian formulation, bureaucracy is not to be confused with the civil services. The term civil service originated from the East India Company which administration was carried on by the covenant servants who did not belong to army or navy. Today, it makes a collective term for all the non-war segments of the public administrative services of the state including the diplomatic intercourse, the working of post office, telegraph and educational institutions controlled by the government. According to Weber bureaucry, today, refers to the sociological concept of rationalization of collective activities. But it is important to note that nowadays there is not much difference between bureaucrats and civil servants. Almost all bureaucrats come under the category of civil servants especially belonging to civil administration. As a form or design of organization, it assures predictability of the behaviour of the organizational members. The bureaucratic form, according to Weber, is the most efficient organization for large scale. It is the most complex administration what has been developed today. It is superior to any other form in decision precision, stability, maintenance of discipline and reliability. For the heads of organizations, it makes possible a high degree of calculability of results.

So far his development of bureaucratic model in India is concerned, it would be discussed in detail in the proceeding chapter. Here it is enough to say that the modern Indian bureaucracy is still steeped in the British system. During the rule of the East India Company successive Governors General of the Company developed the concept of civil services and bought about various changes from time to time. After India's Independence the Government of India followed the British pattern of bureaucratic administration in the beginning. Thereafter, the government brought about necessary changes in the types and rules of civil services and bureaucratic organization according to needs and circumstances.

It is notable that the origins and developments of the bureaucracies in the western politics occurred even before the onset of democratic regimes. Bureaucracies during the phase of monarchy acted as a willing and fitting apparatus in the hands of national monarchies. In the US when the presidential form of democratic government came into being, the bureaucracy remained a tool in the hands of the American President, though the need of neutrality of bureaucracy was felt. Despite the demand for permanent bureaucracy, little attention was paid with the result that even to this day the US bureaucracy is a subject of political appointment; thus neutrality from senior bureaucrats can hardly be expected. However, it is not to say that merit is overlooked in the appointment of the American bureaucrats and politically appointed and oriented official positions. The positions that bureaucrats occupied made them despotic; they began to think differently about themselves. They became more and more proud of their social status and isolated themselves from the society. They became busier in maintaining their status and dignity thereby creating a bar between themselves and the people.

Conceptual Meaning of Development Administration

The term development administration is as new as the concept of welfares to people belonging to various sections of the society. There was a time when little attention was paid to the well-being of people, especially belonging to lower and deprived sections. The administration of government was mainly confined to maintain law and order and to collect revenue for the government. The popularity of socialism opened new dimensions in politics. Advent of Marxism and movement of communism not only caused direct threat to the capitalistic society but also made the working class aware of their rights and status. Political thinkers and social reformers came ahead with numerous ideologies and schemes pleading the cases of the people who are backward, deprived and suppressed. Realization dawned on the advanced nations to help the poor in their self-development under the care and protection of the government. Demand was also made to redistribute the public goods amongst the have-nots. Thus development of everyone became the core issue of the government which needed changes in administration enlarging both its nature and scope. The government began to adopt various plans and programmes for development administration. Almost all states began to incline towards welfarism.

The root of development administration may be discerned in the concept of good governance, which puts emphasis on welfare state ensuring conditions of good life. Good governance emerged with the marked objective to be "a great modernizer, a nation builder and an instrument of socio-economic transformation". A good governance implies that the bureaucracy must work as a developed system "above SALA model of Riggs, exploitative model of Karl Marx and despotic model of Max Weber, Harold Laski, Robert Merton etc. It must win credibility in the eyes of people regarding its actions and decisions."[12] Bureaucracy is the complementary part of Executive branch of a government. Its basic responsibility is to implement the policies, which are decided by the political managers. A bureaucrat belongs "to a section of persons who are directly employed in administration for running day-to-day affairs of the country and whose role and status are supposed to be oriented towards man's interests and not governed by political consideration."[13] Thus, it is obvious that the role of the bureaucrats with emerging concept of development administration or good governance must be associated with the public welfare.

Welfare states are more or less a universal phenomenon in advanced capitalism. It developed as an answer to a problem, which arose during the modernization process. The concept of welfare state is based on the idea that the distribution of individual income should not be entirely left to market process. This mindset paved the way for growth of political institutions to play crucial role in the institutionalization and shaping of social processes. The period between early 1960s and the mid 1970s was the golden era of the welfare state all over the world. The main policy area has been social security expenditure (unemployment and sickness benefits) and pension expenditure. "Welfare state is a country in which the welfare of members of the community is underwritten by means of state-run social services."[14] Welfarism means "The principles or policies associated with a welfare state." So far the word 'well-being' is concerned, it means the state of being or doping will in life happy, healthy or prosperous conditions, moral or physical welfare."

Thus, it is quite obvious that with the growth of socialistic ideologies and movement for socio-economic justice the governments everywhere in the backward found compelled to chalk out welfare policies and adopt more and more development programmes for welfare and well-being of the people as a whole giving much more preference to the people belonging to the deprived and suppressed sections.

The United Nations Development Programme (UNDP) Human Development Report 1998 notes that 4.4 billion people in developing countries nearly 60 per cent lack basic sanitation; almost one-third have no access to clean water; 20 per cent of children do not reach the fifth school grade. The wealthiest 20 per cent of world's population account for 86 per cent of total private consumption expenditure, while the poorest 20 per cent account for only 1.3 per cent.[15] Leviathan has presented an essay on poverty and the programmes in aid of the poor with special reference to the United States of America. He has discussed in his essay about poverty schemes, food stamps, housing benefits, tax relief, direct income support (non-focused subsidies) poverty pensions concessions, public utility rebates and the like. These schemes were adopted by the Government of United States during 1980s with the marked intention to reduce the gap between the rich and the poor. No doubt, the programmes failed to bring about the desired results, but it succeeded in reducing over all inequality.[16] However, it encouraged other states of the world to adopt such programmes to provide socio-economic justice to the underprivileged.

Development in the general parlance is the process of developing, a gradual unfolding, bringing into fuller view, a fuller working out of the details of anything as a plan, a scheme, the plot of a novel etc. But in the term of development administration it is totally related to the social and economic well-being of the people as a whole. The administration is authorized to work for the all-round development of a people under the plan already made by the government. The administration is made responsible for implementing the schemes of development financed by the government. Under the development administration enough scope is left for people's participation in development. Moreover, special attention is given towards the area and the people who are yet undeveloped or under-developed. The latest tendency of development administration is to provide justice, social, economic and political to everyone and ensure that it reaches to all.

According to *International Encyclopedia* a welfare state is the institutional outcome of the assumption that a society is of legal and therefore formal and explicit. Hence, the responsibility for the basic well-being of its members lies with government. "Such a state emerges when a society or its decision making groups become convinced that the welfare of the individual is too important to be left to customs or internal arrangements and it is the concern of the government."[17] At this juncture "every society makes some processes (of development) for those of its members who find themselves in distress." Again, when city "becomes more complex, responsibility for helping the distressed may be assumed by the government."[18] Thus the concept of welfare state paved the way for the growth of development administration making the government responsible for the well-being and development of those who are the bona fide citizens of the society, but they are unable to take part in the pace of development without special assistance provided to them by the government under special programmes of development.

Development administration has at least two connotations. Initially, the term was brought into vogue to distinguish the bureaucracy newly engaged in development functions and tasks from that engaged in the traditional law and order and regulatory functions. But as the sphere of development administration widens, the strength of development officials rises. The second connotation therefore comes in currency. It lays emphasis on the whole gamut of functions and tasks, structures, personnel, finances; organizational interrelationships, control and supervision; communication, reporting, monitoring; evaluation and related processes. It develops the scope for people's participation in development programmes, which play a crucial role in the efficacy of the development administration and its effective outcomes.

Growth of Development Administration

When American funding agencies encouraged research scholars to conduct area studies mostly in developing countries, the idea of development administration was brought to light. The idea was developed to establish more agencies for the basic welfare to the people in general. Like public administration, development administration is also amorphous combination of theory and practice. According to Dr Saxena, development is "probably one of the most depreciated terms in social science literature—more used than understood".[19] Development is defined as growth into a better, fuller, higher and mature condition. Montgomery considers development as "an aspect of change that is desirable, broadly predicted and planned or at least influenced by governmental action".[20] Winder defines development administration as "a state of mind, a tendency, a direction, rather than a fixed goal; it is a rate of change in particular direction".[21] Winder regards development administration as "the process of guiding an organization towards the achievement of progressive political, economic and social objectives that are authoritatively determined in one manner or the other." According to him development administration has four basic objectives: policy making, planning, programmes and projects.

Today, all nations of the third world are laying emphasis on development administration. They are applying both macro and micro level approaches and policy implementation. The issues related are poverty reduction, institutional development at local, district, state and national level; good governance, environmental protection, structural and institutional development etc. The essence of development is a holistic change keeping in mind the progressive political economic and social objectives. Currently, the emphasis is on giving justice to the people deprived of it and work actively for poverty alleviation programmes. It calls for integrated knowledge representing all disciplines and professions.

Another source of development administration is the concept of socio-economic justice to all. This term came into wide use with the advent of democracy and socialism. Though the term justice is not new, it always remained available to the rich people. Plato rightly remarked that if there was any justice, it was in the interest of the rulers. Instead of socio-economic justice, it was injustice, which prevailed among the poor people. The situation changed gradually. A new concept under the concept of welfare state emerged which began to talk about socio-economic justice for the people yet deprived of it. It was the Utopian socialists who were much worried about the pitiable and deteriorating economic and social conditions of the poor masses;[22] they talked much about a new social order based on socio-economic justice. However, they could not suggest any viable means to set up such society. But their thought encouraged their successors to take up the issue, which ultimately culminated into the most powerful political thinking as Marxism, which not only pleaded strongly the case of the poor but also encouraged the poor and working class people to fight for socio-economic justice.[23] Marx and his followers strongly pleaded that that it is the mode of private property and private ownership, which is the root of socio-economic injustice.[24] Hence, both must be abolished and social ownership should be established over all the means of production and distribution.

Thus, the emergence of liberal socialist thought served as a viable way to the growth of development administration. The capitalist governments being conscious and alert of Marxist thought took up various ways and means to develop the sections of the society, which were the subject of negligence and exploitation. Thereafter, a change was marked in the notion of industrialization from private monopoly towards public responsibility. Collective actions and welfare schemes adopted by the capitalist governments began to soften the wrath of the working class. Woodrow Wilson's policy of 'New Freedom' and 'New Deal' policy of Roosevelt proved that the US was ready to be liberal towards the common people.[26] Appearance of newly independent Afro-Asian countries on the scene of world politics and their inclination towards evolutionary and democratic socialism also helped in carving out a new concept of socio-economic justice. These nations preferred changes in society not through bloody revolution, but through constitutional arrangements. The logic was advanced that the rule should be 'entirely beneficent' and "dealing with the high and the low, the rich and the poor should be marked with broad minded toleration and equality."[27]

Socio-economic Justice and Development Administration

The concept of socio-economic justice and meaning of development administration was enlarged. It was pleaded that social and political justice was meaningless without economic justice especially to those who are poor and backward. The concept of economic justice must be based on non-discrimination between man and man on the basis of economic value. It must imply adequate payment for work without any discrimination on some artificial grounds. It should enjoin freedom for all in the sphere of production and distribution of goods subject to the condition of general welfare. The idea of economic justice should seek "a new balance and a new harmony in the present conflict between large national economic and social interests on the one hand, and the individual or group rights and interests on the other."[28] Welfare states at this circumstance became a guiding factor for achievement of social and economic justice. Measures of social securities such as assistance in case of unemployment, maternity benefits and insurance against sickness, old age pension and relief to disabled etc. became the guiding principles for the government while framing policies and programmes for development. A myth was spread that providing socio-economic justice to the deprived and exploited sections of the people does not warrant the abolition of capitalist system. It can be provided to the deserving sections even in a capitalist system by adopting schemes related to welfare and development of the general masses. The measures like constitutional protection to the poor, reservation of seats for their employment, passing legislations in favour of the poor and putting high taxation on the rich may be adopted to provide justice to the poor. If these measures are implemented honestly, the necessary conditions may be created for a decent life, and that can be made available to every member of the society. The efforts should also be applied to transfer economic resources from the well-to-do people to the poorer sections of the community ensuring that the benefits must go to the needy people.

Thus, the changing concept of welfare state and socio-economic justice once more paved the way for empowering the state. The individualist thinkers had considered the state as a necessary evil and demanded non-interference of the state into the individual affairs. It was the ideology of individualism, which had paved the way for the growth of unchecked capitalism. Now the state was once more invited to act in the interests of the poor and control the growth of capitalism. The state has been recognized as the balancer of justice and protector of the interests of the poor. As a result, the scope of the state's power and roles of its government have increased. Since the state has been authorized to look after the interest of the poor and deprived sections of the people, the administrative machinery of the government became more dynamic. Administration did not remain confined to the maintenance of law and order and to collect revenues, but to make welfare plans, chalk out development schemes and execute them in the interest of the poor. The concept of development administration was enlarged. It included development not only of the nation but that of the each section of the people. Moreover, the development concept included in itself sanitation, health, education; small industries, housing, construction of new roads; rural development in the field of irrigation, agriculture, horticulture; fishing, dairy farms, piggery farms etc. Emphasis has also been laid down on the development of rural people by providing them self-helped schemes. Thus the scope of development administration became multifarious. This created the need to further empower the local self government, both in the rural and urban areas.

The rise and growth in the size and importance of the administrative services under the system of development administration has brought the bureaucrats in forefront today. The growing role of the civil service in Great Britain has been the subject of much uncharitable criticism. The civil service has been portrayed as the 'new despotism' and bureaucracy, it is alleged, has replaced parliamentary democracy. Ramsay Muir was of the view that behind the cloak of ministerial responsibility bureaucracy thrives. Jeevan Nair and UC Jain have observed that in backward democracies of Asia and Africa where the tradition of bureaucratic rule had been handed down from the colonial past and illiteracy and general backwardness made it clear that public opinion would be vigilant against administrative lapses and errors, the danger of bureaucratic despotism became really serious.[29] if the administration is not clean, efficient, competent and committed to the public welfare, democracy is meaningless. The countries, which attained independence from the colonial rule after long struggle, are the victims of poor economy and their citizens are mostly illiterate and uneducated. As such, it is difficult for the public to have effective control over bureaucrats. India is one of those varieties of the countries. The nature of the bureaucracy during the British regime in India was despotic. After independence, the government adopted the policy of welfarism and development, no doubt, but it lacked the bureaucratic framework commensurate with its need. Hence, in the words of Nair and Jain, "the greatest problem of the modern theory of government is therefore to devise suitable check upon the power and practices of public administration without impairing in any way its sense of responsibility, efficiency and urgency."[30]

Though in the parliamentary government policies are formulated by the cabinet and approved by the parliament, the civil servants play vital role in policy formulation because of two factors: First, civil service constituted on principle of merits influence the ministers by its sheer ability. The ministers know that the civil servants are more informed of the problems and are experts in dealing with that. That makes ministers more dependent upon civil servants. Second, the civil servants are permanent, experienced and cannot be dismissed by ministers. Therefore, they can boldly put forth their views before ministers without caring of repercussions. Experience shows that in a democratic country like India where people are not dashing and active, the ministers, except a few, are devoid of job knowledge and administrative experience. Such ministers generally become tools in the hands of their babus.

India's Development Policies

India is the land of vast resources but these are still fully unexploited. That is why its people whose number is very large and whose condition is pathetic, need immediate relief works to take them out from the shackles of poverty and scarcity. The country needs the bureaucratic frame, which must be welfare oriented and committed to their responsibilities and assigned tasks. With the declaration of mixed economy as the principal feature of the industrial policy announced in April 1948, it was obvious that the government would need vast army of bureaucrats and officials to manage and control public sector enterprises. The first Five Year Plan (1952–57) envisaged a total outlay of Rs 1,960 crores in the public sector. The result was a steady advance in the number of public employees and the addition of new cadres to central services relating to developmental and public welfare departments. As the years rolled down, succeeding Five Year Plans came into being with the objective to reduce poverty from the country; the number of bureaucrats went on increasing. Thereafter, launching of various development programmes and projects multiplied the number of government officials on the one hand and coming of the Panchayati Raj Institutions based on decentralization of power, decreased the power of the government officials at least at the district levels on the other.

With the advent of local-self government based on decentralization of powers development administration has reached the grass roots level. Different countries have developed different models of local-self governance delegating more power and responsibility. It all happened due to the democratic principles. The state have centralized the powers in the affairs like defense, external affairs, national security; currency, coinage and banking; national and international communications, no doubt, but local governance specially related to development has been decentralized to the local governments. In the precincts of local governments, the representatives of the local people have enough scope to participate in the policy making and implementing relating to the decentralized functions. The local people also share the financial burden for the discharge of these functions by bearing property and income tax to that extent. Merit principles in selections and promotions of the local officials is followed to the extent that it is feasible within the overall supremacy of the popular representatives in the local councils.

So far the case of India is concerned in respect of development administration, it is not behind. The makers of the Indian Constitution were very much conscious of the fact that India is a land of the poor and most of the poor people are rural. The Constitution makers incorporated various ideologies and principles in the Constitution which open enough scope for development administration. The Constitution of India made provisions of preferential treatment for the weaker sections. The Government adopted various schemes and programmes for development of the people, especially belonging to the rural areas. In the beginning, the farmers were given more preference. As the years passed, development administration came to the reach of the backward and deprived sections.

The adoption of the planned model of development followed the framing of the Constitution. The political ideals of the Constitution were fashioned and settled in the course of the struggle for the country's freedom. The broad objectives of planned development were determined to be the rise in the standard of living of the people of the country by utilizing its productive capacities. But the mode of development of the productive capacities and that of distribution of the products of this development in the industrial, agricultural and other sectors among the producers and the legal proprietors of the productive resources had not been thoroughly thought over and settled at independence, or a little later during the deliberations over the making of the Constitution with the result that when the Planning Commission began the task of plan formulation, it began the work on the premise of political democracy, liberal freedoms and laissez-faire economic order. The goal of a welfare state embodied in the Constitution of India was to be achieved via planned economic development, but without the conception of finalization of the plan regarding the mode of development of the countries productive capacities and the distribution of the products among the real producers and the legal proprietors.[31] The Indian planners chose three models of rural development. During the fifties, the CDP remained dominant and number villages were brought under its preview for development. The Panchayati Raj system was introduced for rural development during sixties. During seventies, the Government of India launched various schemes and programmes under the development administration keeping in view the development of the people who were still out of the frame of rural development. These schemes and programmes are still on run.

The Community Development Programme (CDP) was a multifunctional rural development Programme. Administrative functionaries from different functional departments were pooled together with the generalist administrators in the CDP's administrative organization. It was expected to be a people's programme, but as the people's elected representatives were not involved in it, it could not evoke people's enthusiasm to achieve the desired goals. The Panchayati Raj institutions replaced the bureaucratic control over organization, which was in charge of CDP, but the same multifunctional organization stayed. The main difference was the politicization of the principled segment of the development administration. But several factors such as the intensive agricultural development drives symbolized by the green revolution during the second half of the sixties and the poverty alleviation and the a real imbalance removing development programmes, led to the decline of the Panchayati Raj institutions. The development administration phase, therefore, came into prominence during the seventies and the eighties. Small and Marginal Farmers Development Programmes, Integrated Rural Development Programmes, Rural Labourers Employment Programmes and a host of other programmes and schemes were the hallmarks of this phase. Recently, the government has launched a few more programmes for the all round development of the poor people, especially belonging to the Scheduled Castes and Scheduled Tribes all over the country. All these programmes and schemes would be discussed in the succeeding chapters in detail.

Meaning of Rural Development

What is rural development? Rural development as a concept is a continuation from the term "rural regeneration, rural reconstruction and complete development." This term has become attractive in contemporary world in both developed and undlerdeveloped nations. The serious problem of the third world countries which are under the process of development is how to reconstruct the rural areas and rural people who have been living in perpetual poverty from long time. Thinkers and social reformers have presented various models of development. As far rural development is concerned, it attracted the attention very late. Major emphasis has been to industrialize the country. Today, it is being realized that until the rural sector and people of a country like India are developed, the meaning of development is incomplete. A nation may not be called a developed nation until its rural people are linked with means and methods of development. It may be said that rural development means the reconstruction of the rural areas and provide the rural people all possible avenues to improve their living standard. There must be certain plans and methodology to reconstruct the rural areas and people. There is no universally accepted definition of the term rural development. However, it has universally been recognized that preference must be given to do something effectively for rural regeneration.

There are many dimensions of rural development. It can be understood as a concept, as a phenomenon, as a strategy, as a discipline and as a process. As a concept it attempts towards all round development of a given rural area i.e. villages, blocks and districts with a view to improving socio-economic conditions of life though multi-dimensional approach of development. It is the result of interaction between various sectors like physical, technological, economic, sociocultural; and institutional. As a strategy, it is designed to improve the economic and social well-being of a specific group of people i.e. rural poor, the targeted group. As a discipline, it is multidisciplinary in nature representing an intersection of agricultural, social, behavioural, engineering and management sciences.[32] But as a process, rural development means a continuous process aiming at target objectives. Today, rural development has become a slogan, a propaganda and also philosophy related to specific goal of development and change. It is a planned process where all available technologies are applied mobilizing the resources in hand. Various studies have been made to adopt the strategies of rural development. All the studies related to rural development agree to the view that maximum opportunities should be given to the rural people to participate in rural development and in self-development. The government must adopt plans, schemes, and projects and programmes to provide rural people maximum opportunities for self-employment. So it may be said that rural development means "rural industrialization through which a complete rural transformation can occur." It "implies desired change in society both in qualitative and quantitative aspects within the framework in the rural areas so as to bring upliftment of the weaker section of the rural community."[33]

Rural development is not only a mechanism for improving the socio-economic conditions of weaker sections. But it is to be always understood in broader perspective with clear ideological commitment by setting up its goals idealistically and its works towards achieving the same with commitment. The physical targets such as road, drinking water, transport, medical; removal of illiteracy, food, improvement of agriculture etc. are the basic things which need immediate concern in rural development. Rural development as stated above is a multidimensional process, covers wide range of development. It is not only to help the rural poor and bring them up from the line of poverty. Again, it is not only a programme related to poverty alleviation. Rather, it must stand for complete transformation of rural society by making effective changes in the mentality and attitude of the rural people.

Endnotes

1. *The Oxford English Dictionary* Vol. II (Ed) Simpson a & Weiner ESC, Clarendon Press, 1989, p. 605.
2. Ibid.
3. Heady Ferrell, *Public Administration: A Comparative Perspective*, Prentice Hall, p. 16.
4. Bhattacharya M. (1971), *Public Administration: Structure, Process and Behaviour,* Kolkata, pp. 34-36.

5. Max Weber (1964), *Theory of social and Economic Organization*, New York, pp. 336-37.

6. Ibid.

7. Girth H.H. & Wright Mills (Eds) (1946), *Bureaucracy from Max Weber: Essays in Sociology*, Oxford University Press, p. 215.

8. Balu Peter, M. (1956), *Bureaucracy in Modern Society*, New York, p. 60.

9. Gauldner Alvin Peter (1955), *Pattern of Industrial Bureaucracy*, Rutledge and Kegon Paul, pp. 35-40.

10. Rourke Francis (1976*), Bureaucracy, Politics and Public Policy*, Little Brown Boston, p. 47.

11. Max Weber (1964), *Theory of social and Economic Organization*, op. cit., p. 337.

12. Singh, G.P., (203), "Teaching and Research in Public Adminiustrat6ion: An Overview", Bhartwal C.P. & Kishore K (Eds), *Public Administration in India,* APH Publishing Corporation New Delhi, p. 40.

13. Chandra M., (2003), "Bureaucracy in India since Liberalization" Bhartwal C.P. & Kishore K Eds), *Public Administration in India,* APH Publishing Corporation New Delhi, pp. 123-24

14. *The Oxford English Dictionary* (2nd edition), Simpson A & Weiner ESC, Clarendon Press, 1989, p. 122.

15. *Encyclopedia of Social Science* (2001), Vol. One, Jonathan Mikhie (Ed), Fitzroy Dearborn, p. 379.

16. Ibid. Vol. Four, op. cit. p.1755.

17. *International Cyclopedia,* Vol. One, David L Sills (Ed), Macmillan London, (1722) p. 112.

18. Ibid.

19. Saxsena, V, ("Issues in Development Research", Bhartwal CP, and Kishore K, (Eds), *Public Administration in India*, op. cit. p. 79.

20. Montgumary J (1969), A Royal Institution: Variations in three Classical Terms, *An approaches to Development: Politics Administration and Change,* MacGraw Hills, New York, p.159.

21. Edward Winder, "Development Administration: A New Focus of Research Approach to Development" Bhartwal CP, and Kishore K, (Eds), *Public Administration in India,* p. 259.

22. St. Simon Charles Fourier, Robert Owen and Etichena were the pioneers of Utopian Socialist Thought.

23. Karl Marx & Ensiles F and Lenin V.I (1967), *On Scientific Communism*, pp. 26–27.

24. Ibid. p. 7.

25. Bernstein W, (1970) *Modern Political Thought* (2nd edition), New Delhi, p. 400.

26. Cole CDH, (1938), *Socialism in Evolution*, London. pp. 45–60.

27. Coker F.W., (1968) *Recent Political Thought*, London, pp. 138–39.

28. Mukherjee, (1980), P.B., *New Jurisprudence*, New Delhi, p. 110.

29. Nair Jeevan & Jain U C., (2000) *Indian Democracy,* Pointer Publishing, Jaipur, p.41.

30. Ibid. pp 41–42.

31. Inamdar N. R. (1992), *Development Administration*, Rawat Publications. New Delhi, p. 4.

32. Singh, K., 1986, *Rural Development: Principles, Policies and Management*, Sage Publication, New Delhi, p. 18

33. Ao, A.L., 1998, *Rural Development in Nagaland*, Har Anand Publications, New Delhi, p. 24

Chapter – 2

India and Legacy of British Administrative System

India is a vast country where people of different sects, faiths, races and languages live together. It has always been a difficult task for the government to keep these peoples united and integrated under a single pattern of administration and enable them to share the economic benefits of independent India, if not equally, at least proportionately. When India achieved independence in 1947, and constituted itself into a sovereign democratic republic and adopted the parliamentary democracy, several of western thinkers as well as rulers were of the view that India could hardly survive as a single democratic nation. John Stuart Mill believed that democracy is "next to impossible in multi-ethnic societies and completely impossible in linguistically divided countries." Robert Dahl also maintained, "Widespread poverty and illiteracy are anathema to 'stable democracy'—a concept that is supposedly linked with the level of socio-economic development".[1] But these apprehensions regarding the Indian political and administrative system have been falsified. Fifty-six years of successful practice of Indian political and administrative system have not only kept the Indians united but also proved that a society, which is multi-ethical and poor, can develop on the required lines if there is strong will and hard determination. Over all these years, while evolving a consensual framework of a democratic government, the leadership in India has also from time to time "attempted to devise strategies for good governance, which is associated with an efficient and effective development-oriented, citizen-friendly and responsive administration committed to improvement in quality of life of the people."[2]

It is true that India inherited from the British a monolithic, strictly hierarchical administrative structure. The country is indebted to the British administrative system, no doubt, but the latter had no plan and scheme to do something effective for development of the country and its people. During the British regime the poverty in the country especially in the rural area was marked. During the British rule in India some noted cities and towns like Madras, Bombay, Calcutta, Delhi, Guwahati, Shillong, Kanpur, and Surat were developed because these were main centers of administration and business. But nothing notable was done for the development of the rural India. Rather, the people under the system of landlordism and Zamindari suffered a lot. The conditions of the landless people remained quite pathetic because the government had no plans to provide them economic relief. They were left on their own fate. As a result they were bound to face acute scarcity. Villages lacked approach roads, schools, hospitals, and other requirements that were essential for survival of human life. After independence the Government of India was bound to inherit some of the British democratic and administrative models, but it does not mean that India's administrative and bureaucratic framework is a complete copy of the British bureaucratic system which prevailed in India during the British Raj. Indian administrative system is as old as its civilization. The Indian bureaucratic system after independence has gone to various experiments and changes where effects and influence of Indian traditions and conventions may easily be discerned.[3] Hence it is necessary to have a cursory glance over the administrative system of India before the arrival of the British.

Ancient Administrative Pattern of India

Administration in ancient India was mostly based on Vedic pattern. Though detailed literature on the administration of the Vedic period is not available, Kautilaya's *Arthasastra* throws some light on ancient administration of India. Monarchy was widely prevailed system of ancient rule where the king was the ultimate source of all powers. He was the chief ruler as well as administrator. However, he had the political bodies like the *Samiti* and *Sabha,* which were a sort of assembly of chosen scholars who used to guide the king for good governance and popular rule.[4] The king had to abide by the rules laid down in the religious scriptures and guidance of his courtiers. His prime duties were to provide good administration, protect the life and properties of the people and do welfare to them as far as possible. The king used to appoint vast number of officials and administrators to carry on administration. However, it is not known whether there was any universal pattern for their appointment and control officers and administrative personnel. It was Chandragupta who for the first time developed a sound uniform pattern of administration. He divided his empire into several provinces and each province was further divided into districts and sub-districts. He made provision for appointment of suitable administrators to administer districts and sub-divisions. The distant provinces were kept in touch with the Central Government through the inspective staff who used to submit periodical reports to the ruler. Thus the administrative system of ancient India lacked a bureaucratic system based on unity of command and universality of administration. There was hardly any neutral body or agency to recruit the officials on the basis of merit. It was the king and his ministers who played crucial role in the appointment of the government servants.

According to Kautilya, the *Amatyas* (ministers) constituted a regular cadre of services from which higher officials such as chief priests, ministers and treasures were recruited. The duties assigned to them included agricultural operations, fortification, territorial welfare, collection of revenues and punishment to the culprits. There were also *Sachivas* (secretaries) who were the officials of the particular cadre and used to help the king in the discharge of his duties. In various affairs, there was division of powers among the officials and the hierarchy was the basis of structural administrative organizations.[5] A village was the smallest unit of administration. The leader of the village known as the headman was the keystone of the village administration and development. Each village had a council consisting of some adult and popular village men. The village panchayat was endowed with certain executive and judicial powers. Since the mode of society was not much complex, the problems of village administration were less.

During medieval India also, there was no remarkable change in administrative pattern. The kingship remained in practice where the king and his ministers played vital role in administration. However, more emphasis was laid on military administration with the purpose to protect the empire. Good and able ministers were highly respected. There was no any prescribed system of recruitment of the officers. [6]

When India came under the Mughal Empire, the administrative system went under some important transformation. The Mughal rulers took the trouble to improve administrative system by evolving sound and attractive system. Efforts were made to appoint brilliant and efficient administrators to maintain the law and order on the one hand and impelement the commands of the ruler, on the other. During the regime of Akbar the Great and Shahjahan, the administration improved to a great extent because the basic criteria of the recruitment of the officers were qualities and merits. However, they, too, did not constitute an independent recruiting agency with the result that enough scope was left for the practice of nepotism and favouratism in the appointment of government officials and workers. The power of the Emperor was beyond the check and control of his ministers and the subjects. He was the pivot of administration round whom the whole political and administrative system revolved.

The Mughal Empire was divided into Subas (provinces), which were ruled by the Subedars. Each Suba was further divided into Sarkars, Mahallas or Parganas (administrative centre of villages under various Dihs).[7] In the Mughal administrative jargon village was not only the conglomeration of houses where the peasants lived but also the land surrounding it. Hence the boundaries of each Mahala or Dih (combination of some villages) were distinctly demarcated. At the central level there were different departments and branches under the control and command of experienced and qualified high ranking officials. Some of such departments are mentioned below:

1. The exchequer and revenue under the Wazir (minister) or Diwan.
2. The Imperial household under the Khan-i-Saman or high steward.
3. The military pay and accounts office under the Mir-i-Bakshi.
4. Canon Law, civil and criminal under the Chief Quazi (Judge).
5. Information and Intelligence under the Daroga-i- Dak-Chauki.

The Mughal rulers possessed high quality of responsibility both moral and legal and they were truly committed to the service of the people except a few rulers who preferred luxuries and comforts. The administrative officials of the empire were qualified and responsive. They had to be constantly vigilant to ensure compliance with their duties. Greater part of their time was spent on transaction of public business. Since township and commercialization during the Mughal period had not developed much and the main concern of the government was with the rural areas, the administration was also mainly associated with the villages, *Parganas, Dihs* etc. Moreover, major amount was spent over maintenance of military administration because the Empire was large and there was constant fear of revolts by the provincial rulers. In brief, it may be said that during the Mughal period administrative system was tough and tight.

There was strict vigilance and quick action. However, there was no plan or strategy to develop the rural people. The rural people had no alternative than to fully live on agriculture and some domestic industries related to it.

British Rule and Administrative System in India

Bureaucracy reflects the philosophy of the state and government at any particular moment. Indian bureaucracy has three stages of development: first, the foundation was laid under the East India Company's government; second, the Brutish Crown's government after taking over the power from the company, made certain modifications in bureaucratic administration. The third stage began with the independence of India. The Government of India borrowed the administrative pattern from the colonial power where there was hardly remarkable scope for economic development and people's welfare. No doubt, the administrative structure during the British period was fair, impartial and more or less free from corruption, but it lacked the spirit of development.

When India came under the British rule, the purpose of the East India Company was to establish strong and consolidated rules to replace the rules and administration framed by the Mughal government. The British government passed several Regulations and Acts from time to time to strengthen British position in India and increase the power of the British India government and set up new pattern of administration. The Governors General fulfilled the Herculean tasks to improve administrative system in India. They took real trouble to develop bureaucratic system in India based on the western pattern. At first they proved to be not only effectual but durable also[8]. The year 1873 is marked as the first big milestone in the direction of improving Indian administrative system. Before the Regulating Act of 1873, the power was centralized with the purpose to ensure close control over Presidencies of Bombay and Madras in time of peace and war. The Act 1873 restricted the power of the Presidency from making war or treaties without getting permission from the Governor General-in-Council. Thus, a beginning was made for the growth of parliamentary control over the Governor General.[9] The Council comprising some noted members could exercise their influence over the authority of the Governor General. It was this Act which paved the way for the growth of parliamentary system in India on the one hand, and created conditions for controlling the corrupt East India Company's officials, on the other. This Act is also considered as a landmark in the Constitutional development of India. The Act had made provision for appointment of the Governor General of Bengal and his Council of four members. It empowered the Crown indirectly to put effective control over political and administrative activities of the Company.

As the years rolled down, the British Parliament in England gradually finished the Company's rule by passing different Charter Acts. The Legislative Council of the Governor General was given more power to legislate on the important subjects. The membership of the Council was also expanded to enlarge India's representation. It was this Council of the Governor General, which in course of time, evolved into the Parliament. The Charter Act 1833 made certain provisions for growth of sound bureaucratic administration in India. The administrative pattern laid down by the Charter Act 1833, developed into scientific administrative system that channelized whole civil services and established Public Service Commission to recruit the civil servants on the basis of merits.

East India Company and its Administration

The Company government hardly did much to improve the administrative system established by the Mughal rulers. During the Mughal regime the district administration had to face a number of problems. The landlords and zamindars had enough scope to interfere in the affairs of rural administration. The immediate and the main concern of the East India Company Government were to reconstitute the administration of the district, which on the decline of the Mughal rule, had either disintegrated or become dysfunctional. It was natural that this reconstitution should have taken place in the first instance to ensure a due discharge of the state's regulatory functions with an emphasis on the collection of the public revenue and maintenance of law and order.[10] The erstwhile limited scope of bureaucratic operation and the absence of anything like an organized legal framework of centrally supported local authority created a condition, which in absence of a regular control by provincial governors, did not allow administrative system to be sound and effective.[11] Before the abolition of the Company's trade in 1833, the scope of district administration remained largely limited to these functions (trade and commerce). The executive head of the district was the Collector-Magistrate except in the permanently settled districts of Bengal. The collector-magistrate, the district judge and the civil surgeon were three superior officers who figured in the administration of the district up to Lord Bentinck's period. Though predominantly rural in setting, administration had no separate officer to take care of agriculture. It was the duty of the collector to remain in touch with the peasants, to induce them to bring waste area into cultivation and to take necessary measures to promote agriculture and protect peasants against the ravages of nature and the oppressions of landlords.[12]

Thus it is obvious that before Lord Bentinck took up necessary measures to improve the administrative system in India, the administration was based on unscientific line and its basic purpose was to protect the interests of the Company and the peasants from atrocities of the zamindars, which were frequently repeated. BB Misra noted that under the superior district officers there were many native agencies employed in the several departments. These agencies helped the superior authorities to collect revenues. This class of subordinate public employees, in the words of BB Misra, "remained lumped together over the years without any defined rules governing qualifications, appointments, classification and promotion."[13] This statement makes it amply clear that there was no system in the employment of the Indians as subordinate rank servants of the British government. During the Company's rule, which lacked proper system of recruitment of officers, even unqualified Europeans joined the administration whose main purpose was to earn wealth. Most of them settled in India and became masters of properties creating way for the growth of middle class in India. This encouraged some Indians who soon joined the system of profit making and became rich within a very short period of time; [14] thereafter, the flow of foreign technology, modern science and capital continued in India. It was this class of people who put emphasis on development of railway communication in India so that the commercial business could have been increased without much inconvenience.[15] Anyway, all these happenings paved the way for the growth of Indian administrative system enlarging its scope and improving its quality. The need was soon felt to set up new bureaucracy in India based on the western pattern.

Administrative Changes under the British

During the British regime the Indian administration was always treated as something of a mystery. When the British Crown took over India from the East India Company, the government tried a novel experiment in the field of administration. The Secretary of State for India and the Governor General-in-Council were vested with the power of administration that could sanction expenditure in India or alter service rules and regulations. The members of the council were to serve as permanent servants having the control of policy as well in these matters slowly and steadily, the character of the members was changed so that the Council gave way to the Secretary of State's advisers under the Government of India Act 1935.

During the East India Company's rule the collector of the district was the sole authority round whom entire district administration revolved. The Board of the Revenue or Commissioner of Revenue exercised only as an appellate jurisdiction. The police, too, did not have a firm basis or a separate departmental head of its own till 1855. It is only after 1858 when India directly came under the Crown's rule; several other departments such as the department of forests, revenue and agriculture, medical and sanitation, irrigation etc. came into being. Thereafter, the position of the district collector deemed gradually when these departments began to operate under separate heads at the district level and came to be managed by the officers by the separate All India Services recruited by the same agency as that of the Indian Civil Services to which the district officers under the district collector belonged. No doubt, the British government in England ended the East India Company's rule virtually in 1887 by passing the Government of India Act 1858; it had begun to interfere in the affairs of the Company from the beginning by establishing indirect control over it.

Creation of Secretariat and Appointment of Secretaries

Advent of new departments necessitated recruitment of more efficient and trained officials to handle the affairs satisfactorily. The British India government first time felt the necessity of qualified, smart and active government servants who could give better administration. Need was also felt to appoint sincere, honest and intelligent workers who should have expertise in their profession. Hence, the government decided to open new avenues of services like the All India Services and Civil Services. The government also decided to constitute an autonomous body consisting of experts to recruit officers for aforesaid services on the permanent basis testing and examining qualities and merits of the applicants. This agency/body came to be known as the Union Public Service Commission. The Charter Act 1833 had already abolished the Company's trading monopoly. The Governor General of Bengal was made the Governor General of India. His Council had been expanded with more legislative and executive powers. For the first time a distinction between the executive and legislative functions of the Governor General's Council were made.[16] The power to make laws and regulations for the whole India was given to the Governor General-in-Council. The Presidency governments were left with the powers proposing drafts and schemes only. Thus, by ending the Company's commercial activities, the British Government took away the military department and department of secrecy. Other departments were placed under two secretaries. One was given the charge of general, financial and foreign departments while another one took the charge of the department dealing with secret, political and judicial affairs. In 1843, the Government appointed a separate secretary for its department of finance. The foreign department working under a separate secretary consisted of foreign, political and secret branches. The home department comprising general, revenue, legislative, judicial, ecclesiastical and marine were under the charge of another secretary.

When the East India Company's rule ended completely, the British India Government abolished both the Board of Control and the Court of Directors, which were constituted by the Company. All the powers, which resided with these two bodies, were transferred to the office of the Secretary of State for India. He used to be a minister of the British Cabinet in England. He assumed the power to superintend, direct and control all Acts, operations and concerns related to the government and Indian revenues. To assist him in exercising his powers and performing responsibilities, there was a fifteen-man Council in India. The Council had to work under the control and direction of the Secretary of State. His salary and the expenses of his establishment were paid out of the revenues of India. The notable fact is that no Indian was authorized to be the member of the Council. As a result the Secretary of State and his councilors remained ignorant about the reality of the problems of India. However, with the changing circumstances the changes took place in the attitude of the British administrators and they brought about various provisions to improve the administrative system in India. The Government of India Acts like 1861,1892 and 1909 which were passed by the British parliament from time to time with the purposes to consolidate the British rule in India , in fact, modified Indian administrative services. These Acts not only expanded the administrative system of India but also led India gradually towards the democratic country where the Indians, too, got some place to stand with the government and play some roles in ruling India. By 1885, the All India National Congress, the first political platform of

India, had come into being. It was the Congress leaders who played vital role in pressuring the government to work in the interest of the Indian people and include Indian intellectuals in the administrative system. [17]

Government of India Act 1919 and Parliamentary System in India

Montagu Chelmsford who had come to India to find out some novel ways for India's future administration and political establishment, declared on August 20, 1917: "The policy of His Majesty government ...is that of the increasing association of Indians in every branch of the administration and the gradual development of self-governing institutions with a view to progressive realization of responsible government in India as an integral part of the British Empire."[18] Thereafter, he reported: "The provinces are the domain in which the earliest steps towards the progressive realization of responsible government should be taken. Some measures of responsibility should be given at once and our aim is to give complete responsibility as soon as conditions permit."[19] Thus it was evident that the Indian provinces were to obtain more powers in the fields of legislative, administrative and financial. Moreover, there was a clear hint that the British government was ready to enlarge parliamentary system even in the provinces.

This report became the base of the Government of India Act 1919, which introduced the bicameral system consisting of the Council of State and the Legislative Assembly in the central legislature. The Act also demarcated the Central and provincial subjects first time and division of powers between the Centre and the states. However, some important subjects were reserved for the Centre over which the states had no authority to legislate. Highlighting the significance of the Government of India Act 1919, Sir Reginald Copland, said, "Now Indians were to govern, so to speak, on their own. They were to take charge of great department of provincial administration, not as official nominees but as the leader of the elected majority in their legislatures and responsible only to them."

Thus the Government of India Act, 1919 opened a new chapter in the growth of India's federal as well as parliamentary systems and process of democratization of the country. When the Act came into action, a lot of changes were made in Indian administrative services. Some new departments were set up and some existing departments were merged with others to create new departments. Now, the Central Secretariat comprised the departments like the home, foreign, political; finance, army, commerce; industries, railways, education; health, public works, legislative and revenue and agriculture. The scope and responsibility of the secretariat increased with emphasis on better rule and administration where some considerable amount of scope for entry of the Indians into administration was left open.

India consisted of two types of administrations. The British India comprising eleven provinces under governors and local administration under the Governor General on one hand and Princely India under 562 princes , chiefs and estate holders on the other. Till 1921, the broad distinction between these two areas was that British administration in India was directly concerned with British India. As far the princely states, rulers though under the ultimate control of the British government, they enjoyed a lot of autonomy in the affairs of their rule and administration. In British India, the British stood forth as the actual administrators and in Princely India they were content to wield a supervisory and superintending power of guidance which could, however, go to the length of removing a prince from his throne or estate if necessary.[20] Thus the British government dividing administrative pattern in India between the British India and the Princely States, "appealed to the separatist sentiments and aristocratic aloofness of these medieval rulers."[21]

Sops for Indian Intellectuals

The administrative framework established for developmental works consisted of specialized services separate and distinct from general executive or judicial administration. It is notable that the British India government still preferred to recruit the highest or superior civil servants to administer India in England and transfer them to India for two factors: first, the government was yet reluctant to allow the Indian intellectuals to take part in higher and superior ranks of administration; second, the government still doubted the ability of the Indian intellectuals to administer India. This biased and partial view of the British government not only blocked the way for free entrance of Indians into Civil Services but also checked the growth of recruitment system in India for high civil and administrative services. However, the officials for the provinces and the subordinate ranks were appointed in India where Indians had enough scope to participate. Such partial activity of the British government created resentment and disappointment among the Indian youths on the one hand, and activated the Indian political leaders to come ahead with the demand to open all the rank and file of the Indian administration for the Indians without any discrimination.

The specialized superior services recruited in England were comparable to the covenanted civil service while the services recruited in India corresponded to the uncovenanted, functioning on the executive and judicial side of the general administration[22] under the recommendation of the Aitcheson Commission; the superior services were divided into the Central Services and the All India Services. The former dealt inter alia with the Indian states, Frontier Affairs, the state railways, post and telegraph, customs, audit and accounts. It also dealt with technical departments like, Geological and Archaeological Survey of India. All India Services, which the Aitcheson preferred to call 'Imperial', included besides the Indian Civil Services and the Indian Police, a number of developmental services such as Indian Service of Engineers, the Indian Education service, the Indian Medical Service (civil), the Indian Forest Service, the Indian Agricultural service and the Indian Veterinary Service. The Indian Service of Engineers was created in 1892 on the recommendation of the Aitcheson Commission.

The elite services such as chief, superintending, executive and assistant engineers were mostly recruited from England from the Royal Indian Engineering College. In the provinces, Civil Public

Works Department was maintained by the chief engineer who also functioned as a secretary to the government, dealing with the matter relating to irrigation, roads and buildings. Education service was divided into three categories, namely, superior, provincial and subordinate. The superior services were generally recruited in England and the rest from India. The provincial educational services included in its ranks like Indian Inspector of School, principals and professors of government colleges and headmasters of high schools. The lower grade on the administrative side or in teaching institutions was occupied by the subordinate services.

Besides all these types of services the British India government created rank and file in numerous departments, which began to function with a view to giving concrete shape to the government and do numerous jobs for welfare of the people in India. Under the medical services they chanelled the medical services on the basis of All India Medical Services. The chief medical officer and administrative head of the Indian Medical Department was director general, Indian Medical Service with the rank of surgeon general.[23] In the field of agriculture too the services were chanellized and given modern shape.[24] The government adopted various measures to maintain discipline among the government servants and for their better payment and other service benefits and facilities.

Prior to the outbreak of the First World War the administrative bureaucracy in India had for all practical purposes remained free from the social or political influences of the Indian middle class. Its attitude was typically "rule-bound and its emphasis was on administrative efficiency, unaffected by considerations of religion or caste. It stood for open competition as the only condition for entry into the superior civil service and refused to accept communal principles as a basis for the distribution of seats in the public services."[25] Lord Marley's assessment of the bureaucracy was not wrong when he said that in spite of its ability, honesty and uprightness of conduct , it was a cast iron bureaucracy' believing in nothing but the virtue of will and arbitrary power."[26]

Bureaucrats and the General Masses

Since the bureaucrats were recruited mostly from the well-to-do families on the basis of their merits and qualities, there was a little chance to indulge into corruption. They all were committed to their profession and performed their duties and responsibilities for name and fame. Moreover, they were satisfied with the service rules which provided them enough protection from unnecessary intervention in their jobs which ensured their future. There was no place for nepotism and favouritism in the appointment process and the process of promotion. However, it may be noted that when the Indian bureaucracy was tightly bound to implement the rules framed, it could hardly develop. The bureaucrats who maintained a superior status next to the rulers paid little heed to the progressive attitude. They maintained their superiority and command. As a result, the bureaucracy, though well organized, remained out of touch of the general people. That is why general progress of the country, especially of the rural areas, remained stagnant.[27] Absence of top-ranking administrators from the Indian root was another shortcoming of the Indian bureaucracy during the British period. The English bureaucrats, who knew a little about the nature of the Indian people and who hardly tried to go near to the people, did all what they liked. Their attitude and behaviour towards the Indians (especially rural people) was biased. They had joined the services for their personal career growth and not for public service. It is only after the Second World War, some efforts were applied to mould the Indian bureaucracy towards public need.

Another notable fact is that during the British rule the system of the government, which was imposed upon India, was not purely parliamentary democracy, but it was half-democracy. No doubt, legislative assembly and parliament had got the shape, but they were still denied the actual growth and real power to legislate and make rules. Diarchy hindered the growth of real democratic parliamentary system. There was no legislative control over the bureaucracy. It was the Secretary of State-in-Council who was authorized to make rules governing their recruitments, conditions of service, pay and allowances. It should have been delegated to the Governor General-in-Council or even to the local government. The Secretary of State who used to frame rules related to the Indian bureaucracy sitting in England, was hardly aware of the administrative problems of India. Thus, it is very much clear that Indian bureaucracy during the British rule remained totally out of the reach of legislature. The bureaucrats enjoyed enough autonomy and freedom while handling the affairs, which made them arrogant and sullen. The constant pressure upon the government to recruit more Indians in bureaucratic system and made bureaucrats more reliable towards the public and development, the government lastly agreed to recruit more Indians of various ranks of administration. As a result, a separate competitive examination cell in India was opened for recruitment. Provision was also made for nomination in the Civil Service and promotion to the Indian administrators from the provincial services.[28]

Reservation in the Cadre of Civil Services

The opening of the process of recruitment for civil services in India was a historical event. It was, in fact, a big landmark in the process of the growth of Indian administration. The country had the merit to rule India but the meritorious talents could not take part in administration because it was not easy for them to go to England and write the examinations of Public Service Commission. When the way for the recruitments of the Indians in the Civil Services was opened on the soil of India, it attracted many meritorious Indian students to compete for the service. At this juncture, demand for reservation of services for the Indian minorities came at high swing. There was talk of reservation for minorities in politics and services both. The Government of India began to face pressure for reservation of services for the minorities, especially the Muslims.

Though the government wanted to preserve the quality of recruitment through open competition, under constant pressure the government was forced to reserve at least one-third of all district appointments in the service for minorities. This marked the beginning of a process, which made it difficult to reconcile merit with social justice. From 1925 onwards, the Indian legislatures pressurized the government to submit regular report on the employment statistics of each minority community.[29] Such process encouraged other minority groups to come forward with the similar demand, which proved a hard nut to crack for the government.[30] As a result, the standard of the Indian bureaucracy which was set up by the British began to decline with the passage of time. Such tendency definitely harmed the standard of the service and quality of bureaucrats.

An analysis of the growth of Indian bureaucracy during the British rule brings to fore the persisting demand of the politicians for promotion to the Indian civil service from the provincial cadre and communal representation through nomination definitely affected the integrity and efficiency of administration. BB Misra is also of the view that efficiency of administration depends upon honesty, quality and merit of administrators. In Indian administrative system the deterioration began with the process of promotion of the provincial services to the Indian civil service and communal representation through nomination without any heed to the merits and qualifications of the persons. No doubt, such practices opened the gate for representation of the community which was in minority, but at the cost of administrative ability.[31]

The demand for reservation of seats in the Indian administrative system was the result of growing politics of minority fanned by the British rulers in India. The Muslim League as a political party to represent the Indian Muslims had been championing the cause of the Muslims in India. The plea, which was advanced by the leaders of the League, was that the Indian Muslims could not be happy and prosperous until they were given special privilege both in the field of politics and administration. Since they were not only minority but backward also, they could not achieve the required place unless provision of reservation was made for them in the Constitutional framework. The British government, which was giving patronage to the Indian Muslims at that time, used the demand of reservation as a means to divide the Hindus and Muslims of the country. The policy of reservation was made, which encouraged other minorities of the country to come forward with the same demand. Thereafter, the leaders of the scheduled castes and scheduled tribes in India came forward with the demand of reservation for the backward people in service and politics. Such move affected not only India's integrity and freedom movement but also hampered the soundness of administration. Time came when reservation in the administrative system was made for the scheduled castes and scheduled tribes, which further affected soundness of administration. The provincial governments got the power to appoint their own provincial civil servants subject to the Secretary of State being informed within twelve months of such appointment. In practice, provincial civil service men were appointed to the posts reserved for Indian Civil Service even without any information to the Secretary of State.[32] However, the Federal Service Commission was set up only in 1937 with the provision that Provincial Civil Services should be approved by the said Commission.[33]

Return of British Bureaucrats

A serious problem arose in the field of administration in India a little before India's independence because several experienced and expert British civil servants decided to return to their motherland. The reason of their decision was that they were suffering from superiority complex. They thought that they were the royal servants of the British Crown and to continue to serve under the Indian rulers over who they had ruled was below their dignity. Though the Indian leaders requested them to stay in India and continue their services, they remained firm to their own decision. Many senior civil servants of the British root resigned and returned to England. This resulted in more vacancies in the senior cadre of civil services. It created a vacuum affecting bureaucratic system at the juncture when the whole country was plunged into communal riots due to partition of India. For the Government of India, no option was left other than to promote more provincial Civil Servants to the rank of

Indian Civil Services to fill up the gap that further undermined the standard of Indian bureaucracy.

An Analysis of British Bureaucratic System

The system of administration that had evolved in India during the 18th century from the time of Warren Hastings and Lord Cornwallis had the features mentioned below.

1. The district was the basic unit of administration where the district collector assumed enormous power like Maharaja. He was the controlling, directing and coordinating officer. The governing class above the district collector depended solely upon his wisdom and report.
2. Centralization of administration was another feature of the British administration. There was monolithic and strictly hierarchal administrative structure. It were the viceroys and Governors General who had the absolute command over the bureaucrats and they used to decide policies in almost all policy areas like public finance, legal and judicial systems, education, health and even public works.
3. The administrative structure was like a 'steel-frame' and strong institution of a single dominating civil service continued.
4. There was a system of elaborate rules and regulations designed by the British for maintaining control over the decision-making power of their large number of Indian subordinates, who were well trained, with a broad outlook and goals. The tradition was to transfer the Indian civil servants far from the administrative centers.
5. There was provision for permanent secretariat and executive officers both at the central and provincial levels.
6. The recruitment of the civil servants was mainly done by the Public Service Commission on the basis of ability and merits.
7. Service Rules were maintained for them and their services were guided and controlled by the service rules.

8. They were treated as permanent executives being neutral and impartial.
9. They commanded high status and honour among the public.

The soundness and solidarity of the administrative pattern laid by the British rulers is undeniable even as what they did for Indian administrative organizational structure was done keeping in view the interests of the British. RB Jain has rightly remarked that the British regime was the 'status quo regime'. In his own words "It maintained and preserved broadly the structure of society in India as it then existed, particularly, the large proportion of rural society. It did not concern itself with any radical or specific socio-economic changes."[35]

Independent India needed a bureaucratic set-up, which could have relied upon the policies and programmes of the government related to welfare of the people. It would have been responsible for implementing policies planned by political masters who are elected representatives. So long as the British ruled India, the entire gamut of development work was carried out not for the sake of economic development of the nation and the people, but to ensure the control of the government over the nation and also to exploit the natural resources for the benefit of England. The bureaucratic system set up in India by the British rulers may be appreciated for its recruiting process of the Civil Servants on the basis of merits and qualities. It should also be praised for its pyramidal organizational structure, division and delegation of work and responsibilities of the bureaucrats towards the government. Undeniably, the administrators during the British regime were all active, smart and well-trained who provided the foundation for the edifice of the British Empire.

However, this proved ineffective to carry out the Indian administration after India's independence because the nature of the Indian administration changed from 'still-frame rule' to 'public welfare'. The administrative system which was set up in India by the British could hardly meet the challenges that independent India began to face,[35] which is why the makers of Indian Constitution modified the administrative pattern incorporating a number of new provisions, though no major change was made in the basic structure laid down by the British government.

The British government of India developed the bureaucratic framework keeping in view the maintenance of law and order, which was given first priority. The development administration or the concept of good governance as well as welfare state were not a new thing to the British rulers because almost all democratic nations of Europe had adopted the principles of welfare state as a main policy of good governance. But the colonial masters were not yet ready to introduce development administration in the countries over which they had established their rule. In the real sense their administration was exploitative and suppressive, evident from the activities of the administrators both the civil and police during the freedom movements of the people under the colonial rule. There are numerous instances where the British administrators misbehaved with the Indian people and bullied the Indian freedom fighters. Their attitude towards the people who they ruled and administered was biased and partial. The administration, which the British government introduced in India from time to time did every thing keeping in view the interest of the government. Whatever good they did, it was all under the pressure from the leaders of the Indian political parties and members of the freedom movement. That is why the Indian leaders had to work out the new framework of Indian administrative pattern. The British administrative pattern could not be done away with completely because it would have created more problems. The long stay of the British in India and their administrative pattern had become the base of Indian politics and administration. However, the members of the Indian Constituent Assembly did a good exercise by making some changes in the British pattern of administration and introducing new system.

Lack of Conceptual Development during the British Rule

The British did develop an administrative pattern in India, but its basic objective was to consolidate the British rule in the country and maintain law and order. Since the British government had no intention to do something effective to transform economic shape of the country and make people self-sufficient, it did not think of any development programmes and projects. Rather, they transferred India's wealth to England. The British bureaucrats lived in India like kings and princes. Their lifestyle was so elitist that normal people did not dare to question them. Yes, only a handful of the rich and shrewd Indians established close relationship with the British and they not only helped those (British) to strengthen their base in India but also to take undue benefits from them. In other words they were British stooges who assisted the British people to exploit India and its people. There was neither a concept like development administration nor any ideology to transform rural India. As a result, the socio-economic conditions of the people residing in the rural areas remained vulnerable. The practice of unsociability as well as untouchability made the life of untouchable more pathetic.

In the absence of modern local self governing institutions like Great Britain, the traditional and ancient local village communities existed helping the villagers to settle petty disputes etc. The important characteristics of these institutions which existed in ancient India, were that they had been the pivot of administration, the centre of social life, forum for justice, an important economic force and above all, a focus of social stability. But it does not mean that ancient village Panchayats worked judiciously irrespective of castes and social status. Moreover, these may not be considered as ideal centers thriving with the "democratic participation of all the people. Speaking about the ancient Indian village Panchayats Ambedkar said to the members of the Constituent Assembly, "What is the village but a sink of localism, a den of ignorance, narrow-mindedness and communalism."[37] The British administrators did nothing to improve the ancient panchayat system, but to keep it survive at its own fate and resource. The feeling of caste and communal superiority during the British regime strengthened further.

These were the freedom fighters of the country that were conscious about such problems and mass poverty of India. So they began to design the social structure of the country during independent

India. Mahatma Gandhi, the father of Indian nation, developed deep concern about the sufferings of the poor and the untouchable people of India and strongly pleaded their case for regeneration and liberation from suppression and exploitation. He knew that until rural India developed, the work of nation building in the country would remain incomplete. Like him some of the Indian National Congress leaders and the leaders of the Socialist Party and the Communist Party became very much vocal to the cause of the poor and suppressed sections of the society. Mahatma Gandhi who was the champion of Village Swaraj said, "It is a complete republic independent of its neighbours for its own vital wants and yet independent for many others in which dependence is a necessity. ... Any village can become such a republic today without much interference even from the present government whose sole effective connection with the villages is the execution of the village revenue... Here there is perfect democracy based upon individual freedom. The individual is the architect of his own government."[38] Such idea and philosophy of Mahatma Gandhi got place in the Constitution of independent India with the result that the idea of Village Panchayat and rural development got needed preference.

Endnotes

1. For detail discussion on these aspects, see L. Ardent's (1986), "The Puzzle of Indian Democracy: A Constitutional Interpretation", in *American Political Science Review* Vol. 90, No. 2 (June) pp. 258-68.
2. Jain, R.B, (1996), *A administration in India: challenges for Good Governance,* Deep and Deep Publications, New Delhi, p. 4
3. Kothari Rajni (1972*), Politics in India, Orient Longman,* New Delhi, pp. 100-08.
4. Jaysbal K.P., (1943), *Hindu Society,* Bangalore Publication Co. Bangalore, pp. 112-18.
5. Mazumdar, A.K., (1918), *A Concise History of Ancient India*, Vol. II, New Delhi, p. 137-38.
6. Yadgaokar, B., (1956), *The Political Institution and Administration of Northern India during Medieval Time,* New Delhi, pp. 227-28.
7. Quereshi, I.H. (1979), *The Administrators of the Mughal Empire*, New Delhi, p. 222.

8. Roy, N.C. (1960), *The Civil Service in India*, Kolkata, p. 16.

9. Ayashthi A. (1980), *Central Administration*, New Delhi, pp. 2-3.

10. Mishra, B.B., (1983), *District Administration and Rural Development: Policy Objectives and Administrative Changes in Historical Perspective,* New Delhi, p. 6.

11. Ibid.

12. Report of Indian Commission, 1980, Part-I, New Delhi, p. 104.

13. Misra, B.B. (1983) *District Administration and Rural Development etc.*, op. cit., p. 64.

14. Misra B.B. (1980), *Indian Middle Class* Delhi, p. 111.

15. Misra, B.B. (1983), *District Administration and Rural Development etc.,* op. cit., p. 64.

16. Singh Hoshiar & Singh Mahindra (1993*), Public Administration in India*, p. 18.

17. Misra, B.B. (1948), *Central Administration* (1834-1947), Oxford University Press, London, pp. 62-64.New Delhi,

18. Quoted in Singh Hoshiar & Singh Mahindra (1993), *Public Administration in India*, p. 22.

19. Ibid.

20. Nair Jeevan & Jain U., (200), *Indian Administration*, Pointer Publications, p. 18.

21. Ibid. p. 18.

22. Misra B.B., *Administrative History of Indi*a, op. cit., Chapter-II.

23. Home Department (Medical, File No. 41 A) of March 1885.

24. Home Department (Rev & Agri), A Progs No. 3933-343 of November, 1905.

25. Misra, *District Administration and Rural Development etc.* op. cit. pp. 347-48.

26. Morley to Minto, 6 June 1906. IO MSS EUR-573 IP- 110.

27. Report on Indian Constitutional Reforms, Reprint, 1928, p. 199.

28. Misra, B.B.,

29. op. cit. pp. 255-57.

30. Home Establishment, File No. 141/33 (Confidential), Simila Report, p. 3.

31. Misra B.B., (1983), Bureaucracy and Rural Development, op. cit., p. 365.

32. Misra B.B., *District Administration and Rural Development,* op. cit., p. 365.
33. Misra, B.B., *Bureaucracy in India,* op. cit., 263-65.
34. Secretariat of Governor-General, File No. 119/45 (Reorganization of Services to Post-War Conditions), Para-2.
35. Jain R.NB. (2001), *Administration in India,* p. 5.
36. Mangat Rai E.N., (1976) *Pattern of Administrative Development in India,* New Delhi, p. 30.
37. Constituent Assembly Debates, November 4, 1948, New Delhi.
38. Quoted in George Mathew, 2002, Panchayati Raj, Concept Publishing Company, New Delhi, p. 5.

Chapter – 3

Changes in Bureaucratic Framework to actualize Socio-Economic Policies

India is a vast country with rich natural resources but most of its inhabitants have been victims of acute poverty and scarcity due to lack of essential policies, programmes, plannings and objectives projects to alleviate poverty from the country. The British, during two centuries of their rule in India, did little to eradicate poverty. What they did in this regard was a charitable work to help the people who used to be the victims of drought, flood, natural calamities etc. on large scale and that also not sufficiently. Moreover, the development work, if there was any, helped a few of the alert and conscious Indians to grow rich at the cost of the poor. In the beginning, the educated and affluent Indians established close relations with the British to boost their political and social status, helped the British India government in establishing a capitalistic society in India on the principles of laissez-faire individualism.[1] It were these people who having forged close links with the British government and sharing the economic benefits of the government's plannings and policies, emerged as the middle class of India and preferred the capitalistic pattern of society.[2] Hence, neither the British government nor the well- to- do Indian people thought of doing welfare to the deprived and suppressed class of the people.

Some relief works was "carried on at the expenses of the charitable public, aided by contributions from other parts of India and from England". Since the suffering was great and the charity provided less, the people suffered a lot;[3] the government in the name of development carried the policy to "provide efficient assistance for the suffering people without incurring any extra expenditure."[4] There was, in fact, no planning to meet the drought, natural calamities, alleviate poverty etc. If any such emergent situation emerged, "It had to be dealt with by a boy of officials necessarily ignorant of the signs of its approach, unprepared to expect it, and inexperienced in the administration of relief measures."[5] This chapter discusses and examines the Constitutional scope for socio-economic justice, Constitutional base for the Indian Civil Services and analyses the administrative changes from time to time in order to improve efficiency and raise the standard of administrative morality keeping in view the Constitutional objectives for socio-economic justice.

Constitutional Scope for Development Administration

Scenario related to the development of the country and the people changed after India's independence. The makers of the Indian Constitution while providing aims and objectives of the Constitution provided not only a responsible bureaucratic process but also left enough scope for development administration. Though the establishment of socialistic pattern of Indian society got secondary place in the Constitution, it incorporated various provisions for socio-economic changes under the parliamentary government. The Constitution expects from the Indian legislators, rulers and bureaucrats to adopt policies and programmes for rapid socio-economic change and to remove poverty from the country and help the people in their self-development. With the end of Imperialism and advent of democratic rule with emphasis on welfare state, need was felt for remodeling the system of administration.

When the debates in the Constituent assembly in India was going on, Pt. Jawaharlal Nehru reminding the makers of the Constitution said that real and arduous task before them was "to feed the starving people and to clothe the naked masses, and to give every Indian the fullest opportunity to develop himself according to his potential."[6] He appealed the members for "cooperation in great endeavour of building the noble mansion of free India where all the children dwell."[7] Keeping in view these objectives, the Constituent Assembly passed a Constitution for India, which guaranteed to all the peoples of India "justice—socio-economic and political, equality of status, of opportunity and before law; freedom of thought, expression, belief, faith , worship, vocation, association and action subject to law and public morality." The preamble of the Constitution declared that the sole aim of it is to create a new society in India based on justice, liberty and equality. Emphasis was laid on giving more facilities to those sections of the society, which were more backward, down-trodden and minorities. Part VI of the Constitution provided for the Directive Principles for the State Policy, which ask the Indian rulers to take into account the welfare of the people while formulating policies and programmes for India's development.

To achieve these objectives needs were felt to frame such a bureaucratic framework which would have helped the Indian rulers in giving practical shape to the aims and objectives of the Constitution. The 'bureaucratic despotism' which had been the feature of the British bureaucratic pattern, needed an immediate change in its basic nature. In the words of Misra, "Even on the transfer of power the bureaucracy continued to be sceptical about the soundness of a democratic Constitution; society remained generally indifferent; and showed little or no interest in the removal of the wide gap existing between the community and the administration."[8] The Constitution of India provided for a democratic republic with an executive responsible jointly to the legislature. Further, it made India a federal country but with strong Centre, where enough scope has been left to take back the powers of the provinces by promulgating emergency on certain grounds recommended by the respective governor of the state. The President of India has the authority to break up the provincial government and adopt the responsibility of the state after promulgating President's rule.

Ministers and Bureaucrats

One of the matters, which does not usually find a place in a Constitutional document, but which has been included in Indian Constitution, is the public services. A notable feature of the parliamentary system of the government is that while the policy of the administration is determined and laid down by ministers of the country responsible to the legislature, the policy is carried out and the administration of the country is actually run by a large body of officials who have no concern with formation of such policies. Ministers are known as the political executive that is not permanent while the bureaucrats, known as the permanent executive, are professional government servants who have to work under the service rules. The former belong to the political party, but the latter have no concern at all with the party politics. The ministers are in power so long as their party has majority in the legislature, but the permanent executives are recruited through competition according to established processes. It maintains the continuity of the administration irrespective of the party politics. During the British rule, describing the need of responsible government the Joint Select Committee on Indian Constitutional Reforms once observed "The system of responsible government, to be successful in practical working, requires the existence of a competent and independent Civil Service staffed by persons capable of giving to successive ministers advice based on long administrative experience, secured in their position, during good behaviour, but required to carry out the policy upon which the government and legislature eventually decide."[9] The Committee explicitly wanted that the ministers should have the scope for deciding policies while the bureaucrats must be responsible for implementation of such policies. However, the senior bureaucrats should help the ministers to formulate policies because they have details of technical administration. Bureaucracy is such a system which comprises trained and expert officials recruited through a neutral agency. A bureaucrat must be clever and efficient in handling his job without misusing the authorities vested in them. Impartiality is the marked quality of a bureaucrat. To keep them under proper discipline there must be service rules. There should also be provision for ensuring that any breach of the law, they can be effectively brought before the court of the law. However, they must be protected from undue intervention from the politicians and ministers. The bureaucracy needs the intellectuals who are exceptional in their knowledge and qualities. Unless their services are secured and protected, such intellectuals would neither take interest in administrative jobs nor would they perform the neutral and impartial services. To achieve these objectives of a bureaucracy there must be provisions for definite rules and proper safeguards in respect of what is broadly known as the 'conditions of service' of the Civil Servants. It is interesting to note that the fathers of the Indian Constitution were farsighted enough, and they incorporated certain provisions related to the recruitment, training and conditions for Civil Services in India in the Constitution of India.

Constitutional Provisions for Safety of Civil Services

During the British period members of higher civil services functioned both as administrators and governors, executive councilors and legislators. The civil service, after India's independence, had to be confined only to administrative charges as different from political charges and had to be placed under the full control of the government. They had to be constituted into an efficient and impartial public service which would carry on the rapidly expanding burden of an independent and welfare state.

The members of the Constituent Assembly were aware of the fact that due to implementation of development administration the responsibilities of civil services became onerous. It is all because "whenever democratic constructions exist, experience has shown that it is essential to protect public services as far as possible from political or personal influence".[10] While taking part in the Constituent

Assembly debates P Subharayan, a member of the Assembly said, "Without an efficient civil service, it will be impossible for the government to carry on and the continuing of policy to be kept."[11] Brajeshwer Prasad, a member, pleading for the removal of the disciplinary power over the civil services from the hands of the ministry and placing them under the control of the Public Service commission, said, "In the circumstances in which we are placed today ... if the foundations of our civil service are to be laid on sound and scientific basis, they (Bureaucrats) must be removed from the control of the minister..." He further pleaded that "We are passing through a very difficult period. The whole society is passing through a period of decadence and decay, and if we want that the birth pangs of the new social order should not be prolonged, we should lay the foundations of our civil services on a safe and secure basis."[12]

Thus it is evident that the issue regarding giving strong and safe foundation of the Indian civil services the members of the Constituent Assembly thoroughly discussed and debated the issue. They all wanted that the Indian civil servants must be protected from the direct influence of the ministers. Hence, the Constitution of India provided Constitutional safety and security to the Indian administrators and bureaucrats. Some of the members of the Constituent Assembly were of the view that the recommendations of the Public Service Commission should not be advisory, but compulsory. However, this view was not accepted keeping in view the ministerial responsibility. The Constitution specifically lays down certain safeguards against the arbitrary use of governmental discretion. Firstly, consultation with the Public Service Commission is made obligatory upon the government in respect of laying down methods of recruitment principles of promotion and transfer, disciplinary matters and pecuniary and other claims regarding provisions and costs in defending legal proceedings instituted against civil servants in respects of acts done in their public capacity.

It is not that the Indian Constitution seeks to make detailed provisions relating to every matter concerning the public services.

The makers of the Constitution realized that it was not possible to give detailed prescription for conditions of Civil Services. Hence, both the Central as well as the state legislatures have been authorized to create and regulate such services in India by passing an Act in this regard. The President of India in case of the Central Services and the governors in respect of the State services, have the authority to promulgate such regulations. In this regard Article 309 of the Constitution provides that "Subject to the provisions of this Constitution, Acts of the appropriate legislature may regulate the recruitment and conditions of service of persons appointed to public services and posts in connection with the affairs of the Union or any state." It further provides that "it shall be competent for the President or such person as he may direct in the case of services and posts in connection with the affairs of the Union, and for the governor... of state or such person as he may direct in the case of services and posts in connection with the affairs of the state, to make rules regarding the recruitment, and the conditions of services of person appointed, to such services and posts until provision in that behalf is made by or under an Act of the appropriate legislature under this Article..."[13] Thus, it is very much obvious that the Indian parliament and the state legislature have the Constitutional authority to create and regulate the public services in India keeping in view the needs of the hours by passing an Act in this regard.

Legacy of British Rule in Indian Administration

Since India inherited administrative pattern from the colonial power, which was "fair, impartial and more or less free from corruption", the makers of the Indian Constitution thought it wise to adopt the British model of bureaucracy with certain necessary modifications. For instance, the Civil Services of India was a continuation of the Civil Services of the British colonial rule. It was the East India Company, which had given the nomenclature as the 'Civil Service' with a purpose to distinguish it from the military service. The Macaulay Committee had suggested two types of Civil Services— the covenanted and the non-covenanted. The former got designated as the Indian Civil Service and the latter became the subordinate service. After independence, the Constitution of India retained the Indian Civil Service (ICS) and the Indian Police Service (IPS). Besides that the Indian Constitution also laid the procedure for creation of more All India Services under Article 312 (1). Later on the term (ICS) was replaced with the new term Indian Administrative Service (IAS). Thus the Indian Administrative Service (IAS) is the successor of the British designated elite ICS, "which is frequently referred to as being 'heaven born' because of the high prestige and status bestowed upon it by the society and the ruling classes."[14]

Constitutional Protection to Civil Servants

With a view to protecting the officials of the Indian Civil and Police services of IAS and IPS ranks the Constitution under the Article 311 provides:

"No person who is a member of a Civil Service of the Union or an All India Service or a Civil Service of a state or holds a civil post under the Union or a state shall be dismissed or removed by an authority subordinate to that by which he was appointed." [15]

Again, Clause (2) of article 311 provides:

"No such person as aforesaid shall be dismissed or removed or reduced in the rank except after enquiry in which he has been informed of the charges against him and given a reasonable opportunity of being heard in respect of those charges.[16]

The Constitution also mentions of two important things in this regard. First is the tenure of the office of the public servants and provisions for disciplinary action against the guilty servants. Secondly, it talks of the formation of the Public Service commission both for the Union and the State to recruit the Civil Servants. India has inherited from the British system of the administration that all services are at the pleasure of the Crown. The Indian Constitution, too, declares that anybody who holds a post under the Union or a State (Gazetted ranks), holds his office during the pleasure of the President or the Governor, as the case may be. Article 310 provides that "A rule, which seeks to fetter the power of the President or the governor to dismiss a Government servant at pleasure (subject to the qualification in Article 311), shall be void." [17]

According to the provisions mentioned above any government servant may be dismissed at any time and on any ground, without giving rise to any cause of action for wrongful, except where the dismissal is in contravention of the institutional safeguards. It means that dismissal of an IAS officer or an IPS officer is possible but according to the procedure mentioned in the Constitution. It is the President and the Governor who may set the enquiry commission to examine the charges against such Civil Servants. If the charges are established and the President or the Governor is convinced that the incumbent has committed wrong (s), his/her dismissal is possible. Thus, the procedure for their dismissal or removal from the service is not easy one. Such Constitutional provisions have given enough safeguards of their service and protection of their ranks. This protects them from the ministerial intervention or pressure to serve their interests.

Clause (1) of Article 310 further provides that subject to other provision of the Constitution in this behalf, all civil posts under the government are held at the pleasure of the government under which they are terminable at its will. This right of the government is, however, subject to the restrictions imposed by Article 310 (2) and Article 311 (1) and (2). It means the dismissal of Civil Servants must comply with the procedure laid down in Article 311 and Article 310, which cannot be invoked independently with the object of justifying a contravention of Article 312 (2).[18]

No compensation would be payable under the provision if the service is terminated within contractual period, on the ground of his misconduct. It will be payable only (*a*) if the post is abolished before the expiration of the contractual period or (*b*) if the person is required to vacate his post before the expiry of the contractual period, for reasons unconnected with misconducts.

In the case of certain high officials, the Constitution lays down specific procedure as to how their service may be terminated. The Supreme Court Judges, the Auditor-General, the High Court judges and the Chief Election Commissioner shall not be removed from their offices except in the manner laid down in Article 124, 148, 218 and 320 respectively. The procedure to remove them from services is very much tough because there is provision for passing the motion of impeachment with required majority by the members of the legislature.

An analysis of the provisions made in the Constitution of India regarding the service protection of the Indian Administrative Officers makes it obvious that no Civil Servant may be dismissed or removed from his service by any authority subordinate to that by which he is appointed. In other words if he/she is to be removed from service, he/she has the privilege to be informed about his/her charges of allegations and also to present his/her viewpoints before the enquiry committee in his own defense. The object of Article 311 (1) is to save a public servant from the caprice of officers of inferior ranks; other security, which is guaranteed by the Constitution is that no dismissal, removal or reduction in rank shall be ordered against a Civil Servant unless he has been given a reasonable opportunity of being heard in respect of the charges brought against him. A civil servant while exercising his power and authority, sometimes, is forced to take serious actions against the powerful man or owner of a big enterprise or the public leaders. They may level false prejudicial allegations against the Civil Servant with a view to malign his status or taking revenge or removing him from the way. That is why the Constitution has given Civil Servants enough scope for their protection. Unless their position is safe and secured, they may not deal with such anti-social and anti-national forces.

Reduction in the rank of a civil servant takes place where the rank of the servant is reduced to a lower post or to a lower pay scale. Even reduction in a lower stage in the pay scale as an order by way of penalty, would involve a reduction in rank, for the officer concerned loses his rank or seniority in the gradation list of his substantive rank. As regards the penal nature of the reduction, the Supreme Court of India has applied the test of 'right to the rank' in question, in the same manner as the 'right to the post' test has been applied in the case of dismissal or removal. Reduction in ranks takes place only when a person is reduced from his substantive rank.

Thus, a government servant has a right to hold a particular rank, and the reduction from that rank will be deemed to be a penalty. An officer, who holds a permanent post in a substantive capacity, cannot be transferred to a lower post without complying with Article 311 (2). On the other hand, where a government servant has no title to a particular rank, under the contract of his employment or conditions of service, there will ordinarily be no reduction in rank within the meaning of Article 311 (2).[19] Where a person, who has been promoted to a higher post on an officiating basis, he may be reverted to his substantive post.[20] But even in this case, the order of reversion will amount to 'reduction in rank' to attract Article 311 (2), if the reversion entails penal consequences, such as postponement of future chances of promotion or the order contains stigma which indicates that it was penal in nature.[21]

If a rule provides for compulsory retirement at any time without providing for a minimum period of service after which only the compulsory retirement may be ordered, that rule itself must be held to be void for contravention of Article 311 (2), because such compulsory retirement, in the case of a permanent government servant, amounts to a 'removal'. Where the rule does not fix the age for compulsory retirement, but empowers the government to ask the government servant to retire for administrative reason, at any time, the retirement may amount to a removal if there is a loss of pension or other benefits. All these provisions have been made keeping in view protecting the rank and service of the civil servants so that they may serve the public without any unnecessary fear and interference.

Public Service Commission

Public Service Commission, which is the recruiting agency of the officers of the civil services, was set up in India in 1926 by the British Indian government. It was organized on the British model of Civil Service Commission. In the beginning, it was called as the Federal Public Service Commission when the Government of India Act 1935 came into being. The Act also provided a Public Service commission to each province or a group of two or more provinces. The basic task of the Federal Public Service commission was to recruit government personnel on the basis of competition and merit. It also used to advise the government on disciplinary control and regulation of the services of the government servants. In respect of the services and posts which were filled up by the Secretary of State, the Governor General and the Governor under their discretionary quotas, they themselves used to make regulations of services of the government servants appointed by them. Subject to these regulations however, it was necessary for the government to consult the Federal Public Service Commission or the relevant provincial Public Service Commissions on the following matters:

1. On all maters relating to methods of recruitment to Civil Services and for Civil posts.
2. On the principle to be followed in making appointment to Civil Services and posts and in making promotions and transfers from one service to another and on the suitability of candidates for such appointment, promotion or transfer.
3. On all disciplinary matters affecting a person serving His Majesty in a civil capacity in India, including memorials or petitions relating to such matters.
4. On any claim by or in respect of a person who is serving or has served His Majesty in a civil capacity in India.
5. On any claim for the award of pension in respect of injuries sustained by a person while serving His Majesty in a civil capacity in India.

When the Constitution of India came into being after independence, several provisions made for the Federal Public Service commission under the Government of India Act 1935, were incorporated in the Indian Constitution. Article 315 (1) of the Indian Constitution provides that "Subject to the provision of this Article, there shall be a Public Service Commission for the Union and a Public Service Commission for each state."[22] Clause (2) of the same Article provides that "Two or more states may agree that there shall be one Public Service Commission for that group of states, and if a resolution to that effect is passed by the House or where there are two Houses, by each House of the legislature of each of these states, parliament may by law provide for the appointment of a Joint State Public Service commission."[23] Clause (3) of Article 315 further provides that "Any such law as aforesaid may contain such incidental and consequential provision as may be necessary or desirable for giving effect to the purposes of the law."[24] Clause (4) contains the provision that the Public Service Commission for the Union, if required so to do by the Governor... of a state, may, with the approval of the President, agree to serve or may of the needs of the state."[25]

Regarding the appointment of the Chairman and other members of the Public Service Commission provisions have been made in Article 316 of the Indian Constitution. The Article speaks: "The Chairman and other members of a Public Service Commission shall be appointed in the case of the Union Commission or a Joint Commission, by the President, and in the case of a state Public Service Commission, by the Governor of the state."[26]

Regarding the qualifications and experience of the members of the Public Service Commission , it has been provided that "as nearly as may be one half of the members of every Public Service Commission shall be persons who at the dates of their respective appointments have held office for at least ten years either under the Government of India or under the government of a state, and in computing the said period often years any period before the commencement of the Constitutions during which a person as held office under the Crown in India or under the Government of Indian states shall be included."[27] Regarding the tenure of the members of the Commission, Clause (2) of Article 316 provides that "a member of Public Service Commission shall hold office for a tenure of six years from the date from which he enters upon his office or until he attains the sixty-five years of age, in the case of the Union Commission, and in the case of a state Commission or a Joint Commission, the age of sixty-two years, whichever is earlier."[28] The number of the members of the Commission and their conditions of the service are determined by the President in the case of the Union Commission or a Joint Commission, and by the Governor of the state in case of the state Public Service Commission.

The Constitution has also provided the measure to protect the members of the Public Service Commission. According to the Constitution the Commission is an independent body. It does not function under any pressure or intervention either from the President of India or the Governor of the state. In this regard the Constitution provides that the Chairman or any other member of the Commission shall only be removed from his office by order of the President on the ground of misbehaviour. The President may refer the case to the Supreme Court, and the Court would give justice after proper enquiry of the case. Such provisions have been incorporated in the Constitution in Article 144.[29]

However, the President has the authority to suspend the Chairman or the member from the service till the Order from the Supreme Court comes finally. In this regard the Constitution speaks, "The President in the case of the Union commission or a Joint commission, and the Governor in the case of a state Commission, may suspend from the office the Chairman or any other members of the Commission in respect of whom a reference has been made to the Supreme Court under clause (1) until the President has passed orders on receipt of the report of the Supreme Court on such reference."

Thus, the Chairman or a member of the Public Service Commission may be removed from his office only in the manner and on the ground prescribed in the Constitution. The conditions of the service of a member of the Commission shall not vary to his disadvantage after his appointment. The expenses of the Commission are charged on the Consolidated Fund of India or of the State. Certain disabilities are imposed upon the Chairman and members of the Commission with respect to future employment under the government.[30] The Constitution provides for re-eligibility of the Chairman of the Union Public Service Commission for further employment either under the Government of India or under the government of a state. The same provision is applicable for the re-eligibility of the Chairman of the state Public Service Commission. He is re-eligible for the appointment as the Chairman or as a member of the Union Public Service Commission or as the Chairman of any other state's Public Service Commission, but not for any other employment either under the Government of India or under the government of a state.

Functions of the Public Service Commission

Various functions are to be performed by the Union and state Public Service Commission to run the administrative machinery effectively. The functions, which they are to perform, have been provided in the Constitution. Some of them are mentioned below. Both the Union Public Service Commission and the State Public Service Commission conduct examinations for appointment to the Civil Services of the Union and the Civil Services of the states. Getting permission from the government the Commission advertises the vacancies and invites the suitable candidates prescribing the qualifications needed. Today, seeing the growing number of the candidates to compete the examinations conducted by the Commission, provision has been made for two written examinations—preliminary and final. The candidates who are selected in final written examinations are invited to face the viva voce. After qualifying written and oral (viva voce), candidates are shortlisted according to merits. Thereafter, appointment is made by the government. The Commission also advises the government on any matter so referred to it and on any other matter, which the President, or as the case may be, the Governor of a state referred to the appropriate Commission.[31] The Public Service Commission also exercises such additional functions as may be provided for by an Act of Parliament or the legislature of a state in respect to the services of the Union or the state and also as in respect to the services of any local authority or other body corporate constituted by law or of the public institution.[32] The Public Service Commission presents annually to the President or the Governor a report as to the work done by the Union or the State Public Service Commission, as the case may be.[33]

The Public Service commission for the Union, if requested so to do by the Governor of a state, may with the approval of the President of India agree to serve all or any of the needs of the state. The Union Public Service Commission or the State Public Service Commission, as the case may be, shall be consulted on:

1. All matters relating to methods of recruitment to civil services and for civil post.
2. The principles to be followed in making appointments to the Civil Services and posts in making promotions and transfer from one service to another and on the suitability of a candidate for such appointment, promotions or transfers.
3. All disciplinary matters affecting a person serving under the Government of India or the government of a state in a civil capacity, including memorials or petitions relating to such matters.
4. Any claim by or in respect of a person who is serving or has served under the Government of India in a civil capacity, that any cost incurred by him in defending legal proceedings instituted against him in respect of acts done or purporting to be done in the execution of his duty, should be paid out of the Consolidated Fund of India, or as the case may be out of the Consolidate Fund of the state.
5. Any claim for the award of a pension in respect of injuries sustained by a person while serving under the Government of India or the government of a state in civil capacity, and any question as to the amount of any such award.[34]

Article 323 (1) of the Constitution provides that it will be the duty of the Union commission to present annually to the President of India a report of the work done by the Commission and on receipt of such report the President shall cause a copy thereof together with the memorandum explaining ... where the advice of the Commission was not accepted, the reason for such non-acceptance, shall be laid before each House of the parliament." This is applicable for the state Service Commission also. In the state the Governor accepts the report and places it before the state legislature.

Notable thing is that the suggestions or advisories given by the Commission on the matters mentioned above are advisory, not obligatory. The government is not bound to act upon the advice of the Commission. Stating the reason to make the advice of the Commission advisory, DD Basu has remarked that "under the parliamentary system of government, it is the cabinet, which is responsible for the proper administration of the country and its responsibility is to the parliament. They cannot, therefore, abjure this ultimate responsibility by binding themselves by the opinion of any other body of persons."[35] Basu is very much correct in his observation in this regard.

Protection to the Civil Servants

The Constitution has also given protection to the rights of the Indian civil servants. Subject to the power of the parliament, under Article 33, to modify the fundamental rights in their application to the members of the armed forces and the police service, the fundamental rights guaranteed by the Constitution are in favour of all citizens, which obviously include public servants.[36] So the civil employees of the government is entitled to the protection of a fundamental rights prescribed in Articles 14, 15, 16, 19, 20 etc. in the same manner as the private citizen. In the words of DD Basu "If two sets of rules relating to disciplinary proceedings were in operation at the time when the inquiry was directed against a government servant, and the inquiry was directed under the set of rules which was more drastic and prejudicial to the interests of such government servant, the proceedings against him are liable to be struck off as infringing Article 14."[37]

No doubt the public servants possess the fundamental rights as citizens, but the state also possesses the power to regulate required efficiency, honesty, impartiality and discipline and like qualities on the part of the public servant. Article 309 prescribes, "The legislature may regulate the recruitment, and conditions of service of persons appointed to public services and posts in connection with the affairs of the Union or of any state."[38] Similarly, there are other provisions in the Constitution, which empower other authorities to make rules relating to the conditions of the service of certain classes of public servants.[39]

The state has the Constitutional power to ensure that every public servant possesses these qualities and to prevent any person who lacks these qualities from being in the public service. It seems, therefore, that the state's regulation of the conditions of service of public servants so as to restrict their fundamental rights, will be valid only to the extent that such restriction is reasonably necessary in the interest of efficiency, integrity, impartiality, discipline, responsibility and the like which have a direct proximity and rational relation to the conditions of public service as well as the general grounds upon which the fundamental rights of all citizens may be restricted.

All India Services and Central Services

Another matter relating to the service, which is dealt with by the Constitution is the creation of All India Services. The All India Services should be distinguished from Central Services. The Central Service is an expression, which refers to certain services under the Union and maintained on all India basis. For instance, the Indian Foreign Service, the Indian Audit Service and Accounts Service, the Indian Custom and Excise Service and the like come under the category of Central services. On the other hand, under the category of All India Services come the Indian Administrative and India Police Services. Several new services have been added to the list of All

India Services. Some of these are the Indian Engineering Service, the Indian Forest Service and the Indian Medical Service. All these new services have been created by All India Services amendment Act 1963. Moreover, some other services such as the Indian Economic Service, the Indian Statistical Service, the Indian Agricultural Service and the Indian Education Service have not yet been created, but the government is thinking to create these services to make the public service more expansive and efficient.

The Constitution provides the procedure to create new services. It is the Indian Parliament (Rajya Sabha), which has the authority to create new All India Services. Article 312 provides that "Notwithstanding anything in Chapter VI of Part VII or Part XI, if the Council of States has declared by resolution supported by not less than two-thirds of the members present and voting that it is necessary or expedient in the national interest to do so, parliament may provide by law for the creation of one or more All India Services (including the all India Judicial Services) common to the Union and the states." It further provides that "subject to the other provisions of the chapter, the parliament may regulate the recruitment, and the conditions of services of persons appointed, to any such service."[40]

All these provisions make it amply clear that all types of the services, which come under the category of the All India Services, have the Constitutional root. The Rajya Sabha (Council of States), keeping in view the national interest, may resolve any time to create new All India Service. Secondly, no All India Service can be created unless a law is passed with two- third majority of the parliament in this regard. In the words of DD Basu, "The practical incident of an All India Service, thus, is that the recruitment to it and the conditions of the service under it can be regulated only by an Act of the Union parliament."[41]

The Parliament, by virtue of this power, passed the All India Services Act 1951 and regulated the conditions of services, recruitment, conduct, discipline etc. Today, the All India Services are controlled and regulated by rules made under this Act. Since these rules provide that the officers of the All India Services shall be appointed and controlled by the Union government, these services constitute an additional agency of control of the Union over the States, insofar as members of these services are posted in the key posts in the states of India. These officers are, thus posted to the states as per the needs, but they are not under the control and command of the state concerned. The state government has no authority to take disciplinary action against them except that they may be transferred to other places, request the Union government to withdraw them and make complaint against them to the Central authorities. Since the officers of the All India Services hold the key posts of the state and the state government has no effective control over them, sometimes, the state government finds itself in embarrassing situation. However, such provision has given the IAS and IPS officers protection against undue interference of the state authorities or politicians to create problem for them in handling the responsibilities assigned to them.

The Union Public Service Commission has to present the annual report before the Indian parliament. The Constitution provides to review all the activities of the Public Service Commission. Article 323 prescribes:

"It shall be the duty of the Union Commission to present annually to President a report as to the work done by the Commission and on receipt of such report, the President shall cause a copy thereof together with a memorandum explaining as respects the cases, if any, where the advice of the Commission was not accepted, the reasons for such non-acceptance to be laid before each House of Parliament."

Cabinet Secretariat

Bureaucratic model in India starts from the Cabinet Secretariat, which operates under the direction of the Prime Minister's Office (PMO). The PMO is at the apex of the central administration. The origin of the PMO can be traced to Viceroy's Executive Council of the British period. When the Interim government came into existence in India on 2 September 1946, the Council Secretariat was set up to serve it. However, on 15 August 1947, a new terminology, namely, the Cabinet Secretariat was given to it. As the years passed, the role of the Cabinet Secretariat has considerably changed and it has occupied an important position in the administrative hierarchy of India. A Central Statistical Unit was established to advise the ministries and government departments on statistical matters. This unit was amalgamated with the Central Statistical Organization created in 1961. In March 1954, Organization and Management (O & M) division was set up to improve administrative efficiency of government agency and this division as a separate wing of the Cabinet Secretariat worked till 25 March 1964. Thereafter, it was transferred to the Establishment Department of Administrative Reforms in the ministry of home affairs. As the years passed, further improvement was made in the Cabinet Secretariat by bringing more ministries and departments under it. The department of administrative reforms attached to the ministry of home affairs was transferred to the Cabinet Secretariat in 1973. Today, several changes have been brought about in the Cabinet Secretariat.

The institution of the Cabinet Secretariat as a head of civil service has great significance. The post of the Cabinet Secretary has been held by various renowned civil servants. The Secretary is, in fact, a link between the prime minister and the Cabinet Secretariat. He acts as the principal adviser to the PM. He also serves as a link between the PMO and various administrative agencies as well as political system and the civil services. He is custodian of all services. N Gopalswami Ayyangar, in his report on Reorganization of the machinery of government, recommended, "He (Cabinet Secretary) should be an administrative officer of the high rank... and he should be entrusted ... with positive functions of securing cooperation as well as timely and effective action by all departments of the Government of India."[42] Highlighting the significance of the Cabinet Secretary Sujan Singh Khera says: "The cabinet secretary is the eyes and ears of the prime minister to keep in touch with the process of official business in the Central Government."[43]

No doubt, the cabinet secretary is a neutral public servant, but a tradition, which has evolved in India, has inclined him much more towards the prime minister. Though his tenure is for three years, he remains in office as long as the Cabinet is in power. The practice of changing the cabinet secretary with the change of the government is not only wrong but harmful also because it flies in the face of sound principle of administration. A new cabinet secretary's appointment should be announced at least three months before the retirement of the outgoing secretary. This post must not be publicized. It is the privilege of the PM to have the cabinet secretary of his choice, but he should not completely ignore the Opposition specially the main one. A general opinion is held that that "utmost care must be taken to choose the functionaries to protect him (cabinet secretary) from becoming politicized."[44]

Ministerial Secretariat

A ministry is headed by a minister who is assisted by a career bureaucracy, which is itself headed by a secretary. The secretary is assisted by additional secretaries, joint-secretaries, under secretary, directors and deputy directors. At the bottom level there are section officers, assistants, upper and lower division clerks, typists etc. The Indian secretariat system owes its existence to two standards of administrative philosophy. Firstly, the task of policy making must necessarily be separated from that of its execution, and secondly, a transitory cadre of officers operating on the tenure system of staff controlling a permanent staff is a prerequisite to the vitality of the administrative system as a whole. In the beginning, the decision making was vested with the ICS officers but now the same is the responsibility of the IAS cadre. Secondly, the decision makers in the Secretariat were largely the generalists; the same holds well presently with added complexity of governmental tasks. The original concept about the Secretariat was the separation of policy formation function from that of the execution, which was the job of non-secretariat organization. At present, the situation has changed because considerable amount of executive work is handled in the secretariat and several non-secretariats organizations participate in policy formation. The number and kinds of non-secretariat have increased today keeping in view the progressive policies of the government. In addition to the executive agencies, there are advice-tendering agencies, research and training agencies, departmental undertakings, cooperation and boards established under special statues.[45]

The basic performances of the Secretariat are:

- To assist the ministers in the process of policy making.
- To assist he legislators in framing the legislations, rules and regulations.
- To assist in formulation of sectoral planning and programmes.
- To assist in preparation of budget, control of expenditure.
- To exercise supervision and control over the executive departments or semi-autonomous field-agencies regarding the execution of policies and programmes and their evaluation.
- To interpret policies, coordinate and assist other branches of the government and maintain contact with state administration.

Thus, it is quite clear that it is the Indian Secretariat, which has to play most important role not only in framing the policies and programmes but also in giving practical shape to them by keeping constant contact with the government and the implementing agencies. The Administrative Reform Committee has rightly remarked, "The Secretariat (Central) system of work has lent balance, consistency and continuity to the administration, and serves as nucleus for the total machinery of a ministry. It has facilitated inter-ministry coordination and accountability to parliament at the ministerial level. As an institutionalized system, it is indispensable for the proper functioning of government."

A minister is a political head of a ministry while a secretary is the administrative head of the ministry. The secretary acts as the chief advisor to the minister with regard to policy and administrative affairs. The secretary is also responsible for conducting efficient and economical administration under his control. Gopalaswami maintains, "A secretary should not immerse in files and be burdened with routine. It is essential that he should have time to grasp the overall picture, size up the problems facing government in the field allotted to his charge, and think and plan ahead."[46] Administrative Reforms Committee, too, wanted that the secretary should act as coordinator, policy guide reviewer and evaluator.

The additional or joint secretary as well as the under secretary have to assist the chief secretary of the ministry. Joint Secretary deals with the administrative matters related to personnel and office management. A deputy secretary has to act on behalf of the secretary through the joint secretary. Under Secretary assists the deputy secretary and joint secretary in the disposal of government business and have charge of a branch in a ministry. In the secretariat to assist the different cadres of the secretaries there are various assistants from section officers to lower division clerks, peons and Chowkidar. Each section is headed by a section officer who supervises the work of dealing hands. Generally, there are two deputy secretaries under a joint secretary and two under secretaries under a deputy secretary. The functions of the office are divided into two broad categories i.e. (*a*) functions to be carried out automatically on any case sent to the office without specific direction and *(b)* functions to be performed only on the directions of an officer.

The IAS officers are recruited by the Union Public Service Commission on the basis of competition and allotted to the provincial governments. Their service rules and conducts are prepared by the Central government. These officers serve in the provinces concerned, but they are directly responsible to the Central government. They are deployed in the provinces on the basis of needs and willingness of the provincial governments and play vital role in provincial administration. They have direct link with the field officers and control the officers deployed in the field headquarters of the state. Nowadays, a new system has emerged wherein the officers selected by the state Public Service Commission are promoted to the rank of the IAS. However, the quota for such promotion is fixed. Again provision has been made to reserve some seats for the scheduled castes and scheduled tribes and backward classes. All the secretaries of the Central and provincial cadres are IAS officers.

Social Change and Development Administration

As stated above the makers of the India Constitution had left enough scope for growth of socialistic principles in the country. The forces that were directly concerned with the socialistic pattern of society in India got strength gradually. They became more active and began to pressurize the government to adopt policies and programmes for the people who were yet socially and economically backward and suppressed and deprived of the benefits of the Indian planning. On the other hand, the growing consciousness of the Indian electorate made them to take active participation in party politics, which compelled the government to adopt more progressive policies and programmes in favour of the poor and backward people. The government, thereafter, became more alert and conscious. It became unavoidable for the government to change its traditional trend in regard to social change and economic progress and prosperity of the poor and backward people.

Indira Gandhi, during seventies of the last century, became pioneer in this regard and appeared as a *messiah* to help the poor and deprived sections of the people. Her government adopted various policies and programmes to help the poor and improve their living standard. Her government directed the Planning Commission to change its earlier stand and prepare effective plans to canalize the funds for alleviating poverty from the country. Thereafter, the Central government directed all the state governments to adopt and implement policies and programmers for economic development of the people and help the needy sections by giving especial emphasis. A number of centrally sponsored development plans and programmes were launched all over the country supported with sufficient funds. All these happenings demanded active involvement of the Indian bureaucrats right from top to the lower level on the one hand, and active people's participation in preparation of plans from the grass roots level and their implementation in the rural areas.

The gradual shift of emphasis in favour of the positive functions of the states tended to reduce the position of the district collectors from virtual custodian of sovereign power to a mere coordinator of official functions in his district. But since social change did not keep pace with political progress and administrative transformation, the importance of maintenance of administration did not diminish to the extent demanded by development administration. In the words of BB Misra, "While the need for the generalist administrator remained undiminished, the exigencies of the development administration dictated the necessity of specialization, especially in the post-independence period when the volume and variety of development activity underwent a sudden spurt."[47] Keeping in view the development administration and giving more preference to the sections of the people belonging to the poor and backward classes, numerous changes have been brought in the cadre of Indian Administrative Service. Changes have been made in the age group of civil officers. These changes have helped the Indian rulers to bring changes in social and economic development of the neglected and deprived class even as these changes have enabled unscrupulous elements of the society to enrich them by indulging into mass corruption and mismanagement of the funds provided by the government for the poor and backward sections of the society. The aims and objectives enshrined in the preamble of the Constitution and also in the Directive Principles of the State Policy have not been fulfilled. There are various factors and constraints which are responsible for increasing gap between the rich and the poor. All these matters have been discussed in the succeeding chapters.

Endnotes

1. Misra, B.B., (1983), *District Administration and Rural Development,* OUP, New Delhi, p. 64.
2. ————————, (1974), *The Indian Middle Class,* OUP, New Delhi, pp. 104-07
3. See Famine Commission Report, Part-I, Para 47-49, New Delhi, 1980,
4. Ibid. Part-I, Para- 61.

5. Taken from the Report of the Commissioners appointed to enquire into the Famine in Bengal and Orissa, p. 13
6. *Constituent Assembly Debates*, Vol. II, New Delhi, 1947, p. 316.
7. Ibid. Vol. I, No. 5, "Text of Resolution", Clause 5, New Delhi, 1947, p. 60.
8. Misra, B. B., (1976), *Government and Bureaucracy in India*-1947-1976, New Delhi, Preface p. (i).
9. Joint Select Committee Report -1933-34, Col. I, Para- 276.
10. Quoted in Nair Jeevan & Jain U.C., (2000), *The Indian Bureaucratic System,* Pointer Publisher, Jaipur, p. 85.
11. Ibid, p. 85.
12. Ibid., p. 86.
13. Basu D.D. (1977), *Constitutional Law of India*, New Delhi, p. 35.
14. Lata Swarn, (2003), "Indian Bureaucracy since Liberalization", in *Public Administration in India: Current Perspective,* edited by Bhartwal C.P, and Kishore, K., APH Publishing House, New Delhi, p. 92.
15. Basu D.D.,(1977), *Constitutional Law of India,* Article 311 (I) op. cit. p. 364.
16. Ibid.
17. Ibid. pp. 364-65.
18. *Purusotam* v *Union of India*- A, 1968, SC 300 (34). Also *Khemkaran* v *Union of India* 1968, Sc 300 (34).
19. *Sitla* v, *North Eastern Railway,* A I R 1966, SC 1197.
20. *State of Uttar Pradesh* v *Sughar,* A I R 1976, SC 423.
21. *State of Bihar* v *A I R,* 1971 Sc 1011
22. Basu D.D. (1977), *Constitutional Law of India*, op. cit., p. 393.
23. Ibid.
24. Ibid.
25. Ibid.
26. Ibid.
27. Ibid.
28. Ibid.
29. Article 144 and 145 of the Constitution of India in D.D. Basu, *Constitutional Law of India*, op. cit., pp. 195-96.

30. Basu D.D (1978), *An Introduction to the Constitution of India*, New Delhi, p. 326.
31. See Article 320 of the Indian Constitution.
32. See Article 321 of the Indian Constitution.
33. See Article 322 of the Indian Constitution.
34. See Article 320 of the Indian Constitution.
35. Basu D.D (1978) *An Introduction to the Constitution of India*, op. cit., p.329.
36. *Kameshwer* v *State of Bihar* A I R 1962, SC 1160.
37. Basu D.D (1978), *An Introduction to the Constitution of India*, op. cit., p. 331.
38. Basu, D.D., *Constitutional Law of India*, op. cit., p. 361.
39. Article 98 and 187 of the Indian Constitution give detail provisions for the services of the public servants of India.
40. See Article 312 of the Indian Constitution.
41. Basu D.D (1978) *An Introduction to the Constitution of India*, op. cit., p.330.
42. Quoted in Singh Hoshiar and Singh M, (1993), *Public Administration in India: Theory and Practice,* New Delhi. p. 197.
43. *Times of India*, 7 October 1991.
44. *The Indian Express,* 26 July 1972.
45. Report of A R C, Study Team on Machinery of Government of India and Procedure of Work, (1967), New Delhi, pp. 26-28.
46. Ayyanger Report of Reorganization of Machinery (1949), New Delhi, 1957, Para- 14.
47. Misra, B.B., *Government and Bureaucracy in India*, op. cit., p. 236.

Chapter – 4

Policies and Programmes for Rural Development and Changes in Bureaucracy

Development administration got prominence with rise and growth of welfare state. It has already been discussed that the concept of development administration is very much related with democratic and socialistic spirit. With the spread of democratic and socialistic principles the demand of public welfare assumed priority and prominence all over the world. As a result, the governments—socialist or capitalist— restructured the administrative structure, assumed the responsibility to do more and more public welfare by preparing planning and schemes at micro level for people's development. The scope for people's participation in preparation of planning from the grass roots level and implementation of various development programmes and projects expanded. Need was also felt to decentralize the power and assign the local administrative institutions and their controlling officers greater responsibility in preparation of plans and execution of development schemes and programmes. As per the declared goal of the Indian constitution to provide economic and social justice to the weaker and down-trodden sections of the people, the government was forced to expand scope of development administration by launching various development programmes, schemes and projects all over the country. Consequently, it opened wide scope for the people not only to secure economic benefits but also to participate directly in development administration on the one hand, and increased the significance and responsibility of bureaucracy, on the other. The power was decentralized and the administrative machinery was modified, which brought the government officials nearer to the people and enabled them to collaborate with the administrators in framing new plans, schemes and projects and give them practical shape. The nature of the bureaucracy, which was despotic, began to change into responsible and responsive. But emergence of corruption among the officers and ignorance as well as unawareness of the rural mass led by the selfish political elites, could hardly allow achieving the purpose. This chapter discusses the growth of development administration in India and critically examines the constraints related to development administration.

Conditions of Rural India

India is a vast country inhabited mostly by the farmers and workers. The condition of the rural India, which forms the greater part of the country, has been the subject of negligence and exploitation. Nearly 76 per cent of people live in rural areas depending mostly on agriculture and manual works of different types. Despite the fact that the government abolished the system of landlordism and made the tenants real owner of the land, but in absence of proper irrigational planning, modern scientific agricultural methodology and advanced rural communication the conditions of the farmers remained lamentable. So far the condition of the rural poor was concerned, in absence of proper means of livelihood, it was sympathetic and vulnerable. The affluent families exploited their labour and forced them to work for little ways that also not in cash, but in kinds. The rural workers had no means to earn their livelihood except selling out their labour at cheap rate. Moreover, due to lack of proper works they had to remain idle without work for months in a year.

What the country needed immediately was to take up decisive measure to help rural development. The meaning of rural development is to improve the lot of people living outside the urban areas. In the words of P N Singh rural development "takes into account the forward and backward linkages between the rural and urban areas. Its main thrust is on development of rural people as an individual as well as a member of village community, and the community as a whole."[1] The major thrust of rural development consists in "fuller use of resources and skills, modernization of farming, regeneration of agricultural allied activities, institution building to fulfill the local needs, eradication of development problems and improvement in health and education."[2] Thus, it is obvious that rural development is multidimensional in nature.

Assertions of Poverty removal during Freedom Movement

During the British rule in India a few conscious and rich Indian households were the beneficiaries of the British economic policy had emerged the dominating force in the country. It was these elements who became active after India's independence and began to apply efforts to get maximum benefits of the Indian economic policies. It was these forces who had gone near to the British people and their rule in India with a view to obtain maximum gain of the changing situation. They emerged as a middle class or Indian bourgeois who accumulated enormous wealth. They were landlords, traders and financiers Independent India inherited an economic system of "parasitic exploitation that sustained stagnation while accentuating the unevenness of income distribution and level of living."[3] Both nobles and feudal chiefs who had emerged during the British period were present and problem was how to save the country from their exploitation of the general mass. In the words of AR Desai "The survival of the remnants (exploitative elements) of old classes, even though existing in modified form alongside the new classes, made the Indian society a complicated organism with extremely variegated and antagonistic social forces struggling for their respective interests within it."[4] On the other hand, the Indian working class who had neither capital nor skill except the manual labour remained deprived of the economic benefits. The economic conditions of these people including peasantry and rural and urban labourers went on deteriorating due to exploitative development schemes adopted by the British government and supported by the Indian middle class.[5]

During the freedom movement, besides the communists there were several leaders even in the Indian National Congress who had been pleading the case of the people who were the victims of exploitation and sufferings. Even Pt Jawaharlal Nehru championed the cause of the poor and pleaded their case very strongly at the public platforms. In 1929, Lala Lajapat Rai, the veteran Congress leader, speaking about the causes of the miserable conditions of the poor farmers, said that "they were being robbed by the classes in possession of means of production and distribution."[6] Thereafter some noted Congress leaders became vocal about the cause of poverty of the peasants and the poor people. As a result, the Indian National Congress changed its traditional attitude towards the poor classes and began to express its concern for the poor from its national platform. In the words of Chandrika Singh, "The changed attitude of the Indian National congress in regard to the peasantry and workers bore the testimony in the Lahore and Karachi sessions of the Congress held in 1929 and 1931 respectively."[7]

In 1929, the All India Congress Committee on the recommendation of the Congress Committee of Uttar Pradesh, passed the resolution wherein it made the existing economic structure of the society responsible for the "dire poverty and misery of the Indian people." Hence, the Committee recommended "to make drastic changes in the present economic and social structure of the society and remove the gross inequalties."[8] At the Karachi session, the All India Congress Committee passed the resolution on Fundamental Rights and Economic policy which provided several provisions for the improvement of the deteriorating conditions of the poor.[9] With emergence of the Socialist Congress and the Communist Party in India during the freedom struggle the talk about the poor and causes of their poverty got more prominence. The communist and socialist leaders began to talk about changing Indian society from the capitalistic pattern to the socialistic one after getting independence. Even some of the Congress leaders belonging to the leftist group raised the voices against the rich and affluent Indian classes who were not hesitant to exploit the poor for their own interests. Mahatma Gandhi talked a lot about liberation of the backward and untouchable people who he preferred to call *'harijans'*. All these resulted in creation of Labour Union, Trade Union and Peasants Union that emphasized the cause of the poor and demanded changes in their socio-economic conditions.

As the days of the freedom of the country began to come near, the Indian leaders who evinced keen concern for the poor and deprived sections became more and more talkative. The leftist leaders of the Indian National Congress talked of promises to improve the economic and social lot of the Indian poor soon after getting independence. Such talk and move of the leaders who were fighting for India's freedom motivated the rural people to take active part in the freedom movement on the one hand and created hope and aspirations in the minds of millions of the poor people, on the other. It was expected that there would be great social change in India after independence.

Congress Government Efforts to Help the Poor

After India's independence, the Indian National Congress availed the opportunity to form the government at both the levels—centre and state—all over the country. Now it was the prime duty and responsibility of the Congress leaders to take decisive steps to help the poor and liberate them from shackles of poverty and exploitation. Thus, it is obvious that the problem before the leaders of the Indian National Congress who took over power from the British were acute and serious. The poor people were expecting a lot from the ruling Congress. They were expecting the economic policies in favour of the people who were poor, down-trodden, exploited, suppressed and deprived. The government needed policies and programmes in favour of the poor and exploited people and also determination to remove poverty from the country and enable the millions of the poor masses to stand on their own feet by participating in self-development programmes. The government had to fulfill the promises and assurances, which their leaders had made to the people during the phase of freedom struggle.

The Congress government of India accepted the challenge and decided to divert the funds towards all-round development of the people and the country through the process of Five Year Plans. The government constituted the agencies like the Planning Commission, The National Development Council, and the Committee on Plan Projects, the Research Programmes Committee, the Programme Evaluation Organization, the panel of Economists and the various institutes of public administration. The leaders of the Congress Party who were in power now developed certain developing structures. They all began to play allotted roles in the field of development.

Advent of Community Development Programme

In the process of planned development in India one of the most arduous tasks has been the rural development and alleviation of poverty. Under such notion the government of India introduced the Community Development Programme (CDP), National Extension Service (NES) and Panchayati Raj Institution (PRI) with special intention to help the farmers and remove poverty from the rural areas. Development through planning began from 1952 under the care and control of the Planning Commission. The problem before the Planning Commission was to consider the issues relating to how much to save, where to invest and in what forms to invest.[10] In the beginning, much attention was paid to develop industrial set-up related to railways, mining, iron, steel, etc. However, the government adopted some schemes to help the farmers and improve the agricultural products.

There are three phases of rural development administration in the country. These are the Community Development phase during the fifties, the Panhcyati Raj phase during the sixties and the development administration phase during the seventies and the eighties, which is still running. However, it does not mean that this chronological divide succeeded each other. The economic development Programme was in its heyday during the fifties, but the influence of its philosophy still continued. The Community Development programme, which was launched in 1952 with the marked objective to have "considerable increase in agricultural products and more, especially production of foodgrains and development of villages and small scale industries,"[11] was the first experience of the government in the field of rural development.

The launching of the Community Development Programme was the result of Pt Jawaharlal Nehru's insistence on village development and the recommendations of the Grow More Food Enquiry Committee to have a wider plan for development of village life in various aspects and to reorganize the government administrative machinery and to equip it for the efficient discharge of its duties towards making India a welfare state. The Planning Commission under the chairmanship of Pt Nehru suggested the government to take active interest in providing advice, supply needs for better cultivation and grant loans to the farmers. In response to it the government launched nationwide CDP. Pt Nehru wanted that the people of India must participate in developmental programmes from the grassroots level under the guidance and supervision of the government officials. He realized the significance of the high officials in directing, leading, organizing and coordinating the CDP. He wanted a change in the attitude of the Indian bureaucrats. He wished that the top officials of India should not consider themselves as superior to the people. Though Nehru insisted on the absence of the bureaucratic spirit and tendency in the operations of the CDP, he realized the inevitable presence of a hierarchy in the administrative services manning the CDP. He also admitted that "those who are more trained, who have given more thought to the problems and might be considered, to some extent, especially suited to that kind of work are better qualified for thinking and giving the lead." At the same time he also desired that the officials in the secretariat and the higher echelons of the administration should not merely advise the people at the ground level, but they should participate in "doing things".[12]

It appears that Pt Nehru while giving effect to the CDP, liked neither to avoid direct involvement of high government officials in the CDP nor did he allow the rural people to take part in development scheme in the absence of the bureaucrats. It was that dilemma, which made the officials reluctant to take active part in working of CDP. During his phase of administration the bureaucrats hardly took active part in rural development because the habit and attitude, which they had adopted from the British style of administration, had not changed. As a result, the objectives behind launching of the CDP could not be achieved as it was expected.

The basic objectives of the CDP were as under:

- Area development with a minimum all-round progress.
- Self-help Programme.
- Development of the whole community with special emphasis to give preference to the weaker and underprivileged sections for self development.[13]

In 1956, a new ministry, namely, the ministry of community development came into being, which widened the scope of CDP, and established many development blocks in various parts of the country, which linked a number of the rural people with local administration. Later on, a new scheme called 'National Extension Service' (NES) was introduced and a coordinating officer designated as the Block Development Officer (BDO) was provided to each block with the assignment to guide and control the village development schemes. The BDO was supported with various types of technical and non-technical staff. Thus, both the CDP and the NES became the pioneer in the field of rural development.

The success and popularity of the CDP and the NES boosted the morale of both the government and the people where it was launched. It appeared that there would be no a more viable method than the implication of the CDP to bring about desired changes in the rural life of India. The expenditure incurred upon the community development began to increase day by day. On the other hand, the demand for establishment of more blocks and more power for the village Panchayats increased. The government responded positively but it was marked that there was no proper method to control finance and divert the financial resources towards the better utilization for public services. It worried the finance minister and it was evident from his budgetary speech in 1956, when he expressed his concern over "a large and growing outlay" of the plan and emphasized the importance of "the maximum possible economy" by avoiding "wastage arising from delays and inefficiency in the transaction of the public bisuness."[14]

Critical Appreciation of CDP and NES

The major fault of the CDP was that the landless labourers had been kept out of the purview of the schemes because they did not possess the assets to qualify for coverage by the schemes of agricultural development based on the ownership of land resource. Moreover, the nature of the CDP was that it "became a bureaucratically guided programme and "popular orientation was ... replaced by bureaucratic orientation in practice.... Bureaucratic dominance in the CDP, both during the formulation and the implementation strategy, did not evoke adequate amount of popular cooperation."[15]

However, CDP and NES creating new hope and aspiration among the rural people, attracted them on the one hand, and provided the government a viable means to change the rural set-up, on the other. According to the Five-Year Plan "Community Development is a method and National Extension Serve is the agency through which the Five-Year Plan seeks to initiate a process of transformation of the social and economic life of the villagers". CDP was "a most desired to promote better living for the whole community with the active participation on the initiative of the community." The finance minister in 1956 hinted that some more viable measures should be found out to do maximum development with minimum expenditure. The government wanted to view about autonomy of the rural institutions and decentralization of power without the interference of bureaucracy in the preparation and implementation of the rural development programmes.

Balvantrai Mehta Committee and its Report

Thereafter, the government made no delay in constituting a committee, namely, the Balvantrai Mehta Committee, with the marked objective to study the problem of rural development and suggest more viable means to make effective changes in the rural areas. The Committee was asked to report on the Community Projects and NES and recommend economy and sufficiency in the works. It was also asked to suggest economy and sufficiency especially in the matters of personnel requirements and coordination between different agencies at the Centre and states busy with the rural development projects and schemes. The Committee was asked to find out the ways and means for more people's participation in the self development administration.

After hectic tours of the concerned areas and studying the relevant problems involved in rural development under the programmes of CDP and NES, Mehta Committee found that government officials (under the district level) working under such schemes and projects followed a hierarchic bureaucratic trend with the result that even a Gram Sevak "instead of moving through villages, expected villagers to come to their offices for their requirements."[16] In the words of Misra "Those who were expected to act as pioneer in a new venture of nation-building, became mere cogs in the traditional bureaucratic machine, losing all sense of drive and initiative."[17] The Mehta Committee, which submitted its report by the end of the year 1957, discovered that the very objective of the CDP to establish close contact with the rural people and encourage them to participate in local development planning and its implementations had been lost.[18] So, with a view to putting effective control over mounting bureaucratic and hierarchic tendencies and expanding more scope for people's participation, the Mehta committee recommended a policy of "democratic decentralization on a national scale". It also recommended for a three-tier Panchayati Raj system of administration for rural development. The Village Panchayat was the lowest pattern of village administration while the Zila Parishad was proposed to act as the supervisory and guiding body sitting at the top at the district level with the district Magistrate as its ex-officio chairman. The Block Samiti was also proposed to act as a middle body between the Village Panchayat and the Zilla Parishad.[19]

Recommendation for Panchayati Raj Institution

What the Mehta Committee wanted to make the institutions of the rural development more effective and efficient was to give them more power and enable them to work without much interference from the government officials. As it was found that bureaucracy had mounted over the very democratic spirit of the local bodies, the Committee recommended that local interests and initiative in the development works could be aroused only if the representative and democratic institutions took interest in planning and supervision of development works. Hence, the Committee liked to put some social checks to curb the unnecessary bureaucratic interference in the affairs of the local bodies. Therefore, it recommended a policy of 'democratic decentralization' where the traditional executive agencies of the Central and state governments would divest themselves of certain responsibilities and entrust these to locally selected bodies for purpose of development planning and administration. That is why the Committee wanted to restructure the local bodies and suggested for introduction of three-tier Panchayati Raj Institution (PRI).

It was said that the Village Panchayat be organically linked with popular organizations at higher levels and that democratic bodies would gradually take over the general administration and development of districts or sub-divisions of districts. A suggestion was given to constitute the Block Samiti through indirect election from the Village Panchayats. The Block Samiti was to consist of nearly 20 elected members having some women and scheduled caste representatives headed by a chairman chosen from amongst the members of the Samiti. He was to be called as Pradhan or Pramukh. The BDO was to act as the secretary of the Block Samiti. The Zila Parishad, the highest rural body of the district was to consist of all chairmen of the Block Samiti. For the village Panchayat direct election was suggested on the basis of universal adult franchise for a definite term. The Gram Sevak was to act as the secretary of the Panchayat.

Thus it is evident that the three-tier system of the rural administration recommended by the Mehta Committee was based on purely elective system. A little scope was left for bureaucratic intervention in their affairs. The Village Panchayats and the Block Samitis were to play a vital role in the rural planning as well as administration because these bodies were to be composed of the locally elected representatives. The Mehta Committee suggested assigning the Village Panchayats the duties like water supply for domestic use, sanitation, maintenance of village roads and tanks, land management, maintenance of cattle, relief works, primary schools etc.

Decentralization of Power in the Rural Area

A close observation of the report of the Mehta Committee submitted in 1957 reveals the fact that the Committee was very much interested in decentralization of power. During the British regime the local bodies had the powers on the basis of delegation where the higher government authorities had enough scope to intervene in their affairs. The Committee wanted that once the power is given to the democratically installed local bodies, they must have sufficient authorities to deal with the affairs without undue bureaucratic intervention. It wanted "local people's will in regard to the local development."[20] However, the Committee did not drop the idea that there should be official 'guidance' to help democratic bodies 'to avoid making mistakes '. That is why it recommended that the district collector should preside over the deliberations of the Zila Parishad with one of his officers to act as its secretary.[21]

The CDP was looked upon as a primary concern of the central government. The Central Government officials of the CDP administration had been the prime movers and initiators. The chief secretary and the development commissioner of the state government had prepared the blueprints of the CDP for the whole state as well as their outlines for the districts while the district collectors and the project officers or the block development officers (BDOs) bore the brunt of its execution in their specific areas. The interlinking of the Village Panchayats with the community development blocks and the latter with the district organization for community development was not conceived in delineating a democratically elected village Panchayat as the development agency for the village and inter-relating the rural local self-governing institutions to the state administration for rural development for all the concerned works. No doubt, the concept of the Village Panchayat in India is very old and older than the CDP, but it lacked proper organization and financial support, what the blocks have today. It was the Mehta Committee, which put emphasis on interlinking three-tier institutions of the Panchayati Raj Institution. The third Five-Year Plan easily accepted the suggestions of the Mehta Committee and decided to interlink the three-tier PRI with the Community Development Project.

The problem before the government was how to make plans for rural development and how to canalize the fund towards the rural areas. A case study of Haveli Block Advisory Committee by Inamdar discovered that the block budget formulation was essentially looked upon as an administrative matter with which people had very little concern.[22] It was Mehta Committee, which observed that "with the background of absence of democratic advisory bodies or effective self-governing rural administrative institutions in functional areas, we have to consider whether the time has arrived to replace all those bodies by a single representative and vigorous democratic institutions to take charge of all aspects of development works in the rural areas."

The Mehta Study Team, therefore, urged for the decentralization of all rural development work within the districts and all administrative functions except law and order, justice and revenue (land) to the Zila Parishads. The guidance, supervision and higher planning, hitherto done by the state government, was also proposed by the Study Team to be transferred to the Panchayati Raj bodies. In the words of Inamdar "Bureaucratism, democratism and decentralism were the triad ideologies, which were implicit in the development over the shape of the structures and their contents relating to future of the CDP during the closing years of the fifties and sixties ... The Balvantrai Mehta Committee's report was based on these posltulates."[23]

Time had arrived where bureaucratization had to make way for democratization and to decentralization because democratization was accepted principle of the Indian constitution at the levels from the national to the village. Centralization underlay the organization of the CDP during the fifties since its inception. Till 1956, the CDP under the direct charge of the ministry of community development was a bureaucratic organization with the exception of its engineer-head, a non civil servant. Centralization was accompanied by bureaucratization at the national level of the CDP. A central committee used to give policy direction to the programmes. The plan including the CDP had to receive approval of the National Development Council. At the state level the development commissioner, a new administrative mechanism, was introduced to take charge of the CDP organisation. It was expected that the development commissioner would not only provide a single line source of direction, control and accountability of the organisation of the CDP, but also act as the centre for coordination among the different technical departments at the state level, both in the secretariat and the executive departments. The development commissioner would also liaise with the Panchayati cell at the state secretariat, which was under the chief secretary at that time.[24]

At the district level, the district collector was accepted as the captain and coordinator of the team of development officers of different technical departments. His role was to give directions to technical departments of the CDP and guide and direct the activities of BDOs, project officers and other related officials. Since the district collector had to look after other district affairs, he had little time to provide adequate captaincy and coordination to the CDP. The bureaucratization at the district level and the block level was found in nomination of the members of the CDP and in selection of the chairmen. Induction of the village level workers (VLW) and the Gram Sevak in the Panchayats was, in fact, an innovation of the CDP, but their roles in village development were found unsatisfactory because of their nonchalance towards their duties. Moreover, there was many a shortcoming in their appointments. Most of them were not trained. They were neither properly qualified nor efficiently active. Hence, they hardly assisted the villagers on the required line.

Introduction of Three-tier Panchayati Raj System

The government accepting the recommendations of the Mehta Committee introduced the three-tier Panchayati Raj system all over the country taking the state's chief ministers in good faith. This opened wide scope for people's participation in local administration for local development. The structural pattern of the rural development based on the Mehta Committee was good but financial base of the local bodies was still weak. Moreover, corruption made inroads among the officials involved. Again, there were several sections of the people such as artisans, field workers, small farmers and the down-trodden people who did not avail the opportunity to obtain the benefits of the development programmes implemented through the Panchayati Raj system due to their mass illiteracy, lack of political awareness and acute poverty. The rural elites establishing favourable contacts with the corrupt government officials related to the PRI spared nothing to serve their selfish interests. As a result, the CDP, despite its popularity could hardly achieve the desired goal and played unsatisfactory role in poverty alleviation programmes.[25] The programmes, which were implemented through the local bodies, remained under the dominance and influence of the affluent people who were more conscious about their own development.

People's Participation in Local Administration

The Panchayati Raj system was introduced in India with the marked objective to help the poor people in self-development and remove poverty from the country. Hence, it was essential to enable the people to take part in formulation of schemes and programmes for village development. Without people's participation in development administration bureaucratic elitism and totalitarianism cannot be checked. People's participation in development administration means the direct involvement of people in the process of administrative decision-making, policy formulation and implementation.[26] In the broader sense it includes all the activities concerning community life in social, economic and political fields, but in the narrow sense it means a convergent action by which the citizens take part in the accomplishment of administrative services without belonging to the governing or managing organs.[27] According to SN Misra people's participation or involvement in administration can be understood in four senses mentioned as follows:

(*a*) participation of people in decision making;

(*b*) participation in implementation or in development programmes and projects;

(*c*) participation in monitoring and evaluation of development programmes and projects; and

(*d*) sharing the benefits of developments.[28]

The Mehta Study Team's definition of people's participation in the community development was comprehensive and pervasive. It said "People's participation is not merely their providing a certain proportion of the cost of a particular work in cash, kind or manual labour. It is their full realization that all aspects of community development are their concern and the government's participation is only to assist them where such assistance is necessary"[29]

The Congress government under the leadership of Pt Jawaharlal Nehru wanted "to promote a rapid rise in the standard of living of the people by efficient exploitation of the resources of the country, increasing production and offering opportunities to all for employment in the service of the community."[30] The Congress desired that the planning should take place on the socialistic pattern of society.[31] Second Five-Year Plan under the guidance of Pt Nehru was aimed at increasing the national income and employment with greater equality in income and wealth. It stated that the "benefits of economic development must accrue more and more to the relatively less privileged classes of society, and there should be progressive reduction of concentration of income, wealth and economic power."[32]

The main thrust of economic development during the Nehru's regime was to work for establishment of egalitarian society with special emphasis on rapid increase on the standard of living of the people who were still living below the line of poverty. The three-tier Panchayati Raj institutions were adopted by most of the Indian states with the objective to achieve the objectives mentioned above. In the words of BB Misra "Panchayati Raj between 1959 and 1964 (before the death of Pt Nehru) was a period of ascendancy, a period of socialistic efflorescence, which though dimmed for a while by the Sino-Indian conflicts in 1962, continued to receive the directions and guidance of Jawaharlal Nehru." However, it is notable that despite having autonomy and power, the local bodies in the rural areas did not diminish the poverty of the people who were landless and suppressed. They were yet far away from active participation in development programmes. The government of Pt Nehru talked much about improving the standard of the people, but in reality the standard of only those people improved who were either in the government or moving round the government. The government did a little to control the selfish elements of the affluent class who managed to amass huge amount of wealth through mismanagement of the funds. After his death, the economic condition of the country due to Sino-India conflicts was not sound. Moreover, no political leader of India showed the interests towards people's development like Pt Nehru till Indira Gandhi emerged on the political scene of the country like a shining star. Lal Bahadur Shastri, the successor of Pt Nehru, was not even in a mood to run the community development programmes. He admitted that "he did not share Nehru's faith in the capacity of the people to rule them."[33]

Declination of CDP

A question may be raised here as to what were the real causes of declination in the CDP after death of Pt Nehru. The answer is given below. Firstly, the CDP had neither its root in India nor the Indian soil was fit for its growth. The CDP was launched in India in a haphazard manner because America had agreed to give economic assistance to India provided it was ready to implement the block system of American type for rural development. So India launched the CDP but without proper background. Neither the officials attached with the CDP were trained nor did they have real commitment to it. As a result, it could hardly achieve the desired goal. Secondly, various study teams related to the working of the CDP found that its performance was not satisfactory. Thirdly, the group of vested interests who were interested in making India a capitalistic state took it as a hurdle in the path of their own progress. For instance, in Maharashtra, the sugar lobby openly began to put resistance on the path of the CDP. Fourthly, the most important reason of declination of the CDP was the lack of political will on the part of both the central as well as state governments. Majority of the state governments passed the Panchayati Raj Act but their interest in the CDP and the PRI always remained feeble. On the other hand, the Central government remained totally dependent upon the state governments for working and success of the CDP. Fifthly, one of the vital causes of failure of the CDP was mounting corruption and declining morality of the government officials and the people as a whole. Most of the government servants and the public leaders including rural elites indulged in money making affairs with the result that the funds provided for the CDP and PRI were mismanaged. Last but not the least, there was lack of proper finance. The structural mechanism of the rural administration based on the suggestions of the Mehta Committee was sound but no required finance was provided to run it efficiently. Hence, the interest of the people in the CDP began to recede.

Asok Mehta Committee

To find out the real causes of failure of the CDP and suggest new measures for rural development the government of India appointed another committee, namely Asok Mehta Committee, which submitted its report in 1978. Like the earlier Mehta Committee it also put emphasis on decentralization of power in the rural areas. Though its proposal for two-tier Panchayati Raj comprising Zila Parishad and the Panchayat Mandal was not encouraging, but some of its recommendations were highly appreciable and the government accepted them. Keeping in view increasing scope of rural development and advent of modern technology in the field of rural development, it suggested that the Zila Parishad should be made responsible for planning. It was also of the view that members of the parliament (MPs) and the MLAs should be allowed to take part in the planning through participation in their respective Zila Parishads as ex officio members. The Committee reported "We have reached a stage of political evolution where it would be unrealistic to expect that political parties would keep themselves away from these elections....Their participation would make for a clearer orientation towards programmes and would facilitate healthier linkage with the higher level political processes."[34] It wanted planning for rural development from the bottom level [35] besides its emphasis on close relationship of the CDP with voluntary agencies and associations. It liked to create a 'planning cell' consisting of technical experts in various fields to help the members of the Zila Parishad in preparation of plans.

The Dantewala Committee, too, suggested that the planning team located in the district level should essentially move down to the selected blocks and prepare the block level plans in association with the BDOs, the Panchayat Samiti, voluntary agencies and other concerned at block level. The plan prepared by the block should be sent to the Zila Parishad for its final approval. In other words, it was suggested that rough planning should be done from the bottom and finalized by the technical planning team of the district level. The idea behind such suggestion was that the active involvement of the PRI in the planning process would provide a better climate for people's participation in the implementation of the plan. The government accepted these suggestions with the result that development administration at the district level got the support of elected people's representatives and non-governmental agencies. This expanded the scope of development at the rural areas. It also provided the opportunity to the elected legislative members of the areas concerned.

Good Governance of Indira Gandhi

Development administration in India got real and decisive push during the stewardship of late Prime Minister Indira Gandhi. No doubt, the process of planning for rural development suggested by various committees served the fertile ground for planning from the grassroots level. The question was diversion of funds towards rural section. Indira Gandhi as prime minister of India took real initiative in this regard with the result that the country witnessed much progress towards development administration from 1970 onwards. She directed the planners to make a shift in planning from macro-level to micro-level. The planners accepted the multi-level and decentralized level approach of planning, which opened wide scope for people's participation in both the planning and its implementation. What the country needed, in fact, was to go for small planning covering various aspects of rural life with special emphasis on poverty alleviation programmes. Mrs. Gandhi realizing the needs of the nation, and also to fulfill her promises that she had made to the people during election campaign, took up bold steps to canalize the national funds towards the rural areas. She dared to nationalize the 14 big commercial banks of India. Furthermore, she abolished the payment of the privy purses to the ex-Indian rulers despite hard protest and litigation. Her dynamic step invited criticism even from her own party. However, she remained firm to her resolve and implemented her decisions. The Planning Commission of India under the direction of the Mrs. Gandhi's government made it clear that "the current level of inequality is incompatible with our goal of removal of poverty."[36]

The development plans, which existed during the sixties were Intensive Agricultural District Plan (IADP, Intensive Agricultural Area Programme (IAAP), Drought Prone area Programme (DPAP), Irrigation Project Area Programme (IPAP), etc. which benefited the big farmers only. The question was how to improve the economic conditions of millions of the poor and deprived sections of the people. Mrs. Gandhi thought of ways and means to achieve it. In the words of Maithani "Since the seventies the emphasis shifted from agriculture and rural development was defined as a strategy designed to improve the economic and social life of a specific group of people living in rural areas."[37] Under such shift, preference was given to the people living below the line of poverty first time.

Integrated Rural Development Programme

Now under the changed circumstance some plans such as Cash Employment Programme for Upliftment of the rural people and the Minimum Need Programme to alleviate poverty were launched, but these did not cover the whole country and led to regional disparities in development. Such plans increased the gap between the rich and the poor. So importance of multiplicity of programmes for rural masses through different agencies was felt. It was realized that there should be single integrated programme to be called Integrated Rural Development Programme (IRDP) covering all aspects of the rural life all over the country with greater financial support from the Centre. Hence the IRDP in the form of 'single largest anti-thrust 'emerged during the Sixth Five-Year Plan (1978–83), which further opened new dimensions in the field of development administration in India.

IRDP appeared as a multidimensional project, which covered many sides of the rural development. Since it was based on integrated approach, it integrated various development programmes. It stood for integration between growth forces and variables, interacting in an overall framework. It was "an organised effort to evolve the possibility of developing infrastructural facilities along with intersectional avenues in an integrated framework at micro level."[38] Integrated rural developments was, in fact, a "package programme of various rural development services and activities of a government, which were closely interrelated." It was also a nationwide movement, stimulated or guided by the government. In this movement main thrust was rural development with the help to the rural people who are given direct opportunity to participate in various development programmes and obtain the benefits. These programmes included efficient rural cooperatives, land reforms measures conducive to cooperative action among farmers, education, family planning, cottage industries, basic technical training for self-employment and many other schemes, which aimed to help the individual to raise their living standard. According to SN Misra it is an attempt towards elimination of poverty by providing jobs to the majority of rural poor and other facilities towards their all-round development.[39] It is in fact, a poverty alleviation programme, which aimed at helping the people who lived below the line of poverty to overcome it by encouraging and enabling them to participate in poverty alleviation programmes and remove poverty. There was provision for granting loans with good amount of subsidies so that people may start money-earning business like dairy, poultry, piggery farms, sheep and goat rearing, honey keeping, small scale industries, running of small shops etc. It also provided professional training to the rural people so that they may be able to get employment either under the government technical establishments or under the self-created avenues. The IRDP had the objective to help the rural people in improving their health by providing nutritious food to children and pregnant women, imparting basic education to the villagers, giving medical facilities, improving sanitation, protecting natural environment, supplying drinking water etc. It laid emphasis on establishing primary health units in the rural areas. Again, it wanted to alter the rural economic face through launching programmes, which may help the villagers in constructing roads, approach roads for villages, playgrounds for youths, community halls and other facilities. It brought the government and rural people near to one another. Thus it is obvious that IRDP is multidimensional in its approach and a package programme of various rural development services and activities of the government. It is based on centralized micro-level planning at the block level and 'offers a package of programmes for the rural people' giving more preference to those who are still below the poverty line.[40]

In India, the IRDP from its inception has been related to an organ of the government to use its effort to "evolve the possibility of developing infrastructural facilities along with inter-sectoral avenues in an integrated framework at micro-level".[41] The Planning Commission of India once more reiterated its commitment for giving "a practical shape to the nation's collective will for using all the latent resources and energies of the nation for an effective attack on poverty, unemployment and inequalities.[42] Therefore, various rural development programmes were launched under a single agency known as the District Rural Development Agency (DRDA) headed by the deputy commissioner and other officials of the district.

The IRDP was introduced in India in 1980. Its launch covered all the 5011 development blocks in the country. Thousands of government officials were involved in giving practical shape to the programme of IRDP. The prime minister in his inaugural speech at National Development Council Conference held on 3 November 1985 said, "Our anti-poverty programme constitutes the core of the 20-point programme. These will be expanded and restricted to give maximum assistance to families below the poverty line."[43] Regarding the people's participation in the programme, the PM said, "We must evolve the people in implementing these programme. A new life has to be breathed into decentralized institutions."[44]

Thereafter, the sixth and seventh Five-Year Plans laid much emphasis on rural development under the IRDP. The main beneficiaries under the IRDP have been small and marginal farmers, rural artisans, tenants, sharecroppers, agricultural labourers, members of the scheduled castes and the scheduled tribes, rural women and children. Poor family was selected as the unit of development. Programme were launched which created more avenues for self-employment. It "aims at wiping out poverty by providing opportunities for gainful employment and emphasizes on improvement in the quality of life. Seventh Five-Year Plan expressed its aim for "economic betterment of the poorer sections" by bringing "structural changes, educational development, and growth in awareness and changes in the outlook, motivation and attitudes."[45] It put emphasis on such planning, which could "provide opportunities to poorer sections to display initiative and to stand on their legs through various packages."

Components of IRDP

Thus many poor families were involved in the IRDP. The components of the IRDP such as Industry Service and Business (ISB) and the Training of Rural Youth for self-employment (TRYSEM), were also launched with a view to help the rural youths in obtaining self-employment with the help of the government financial and technical assistance. Provisions for giving rural youths trainings in the fields of driving, knitting and embroidery etc. were made on large scale all over the country with government stipends and subsidy money. The Rural Industry Programme and Rural Artisan Programme were already on the run. The District Industries Centers were directed to promote and develop small scale cottage and tiny industries in the rural fields. The District Industries Centers (DCI) were instructed to identify and specify industries/enterprises fit for promotion and development in each block and provide financial and material assistance to the identified participants to enable them to set up units in this regard. Instructions were passed on to provide training under the IRDP and training "may be imparted in polytechnics, school training run by the Khadi and Village Industry Corporation."[46]

To provide supplementary employment to the underdeveloped rural landless youth two special schemes, namely, National Rural Employment Programme (NREP) and Rural Landless Employment Programme (RLEP) were lunched in 1980 and 1983 respectively to provide more jobs to the rural unemployed people. The Government of India sanctioned crores of rupees to give practical shape to these two programmes.[47] Each admitted trainee was given sufficient amount of money to complete the course.[48] Allocation of Rs 230 crores was made as Central assistance under NREP for the Year 1985 only. A quality of 2.3 lakhs MTs of foodgrains was also allotted for distribution among workers at the rate of one kg per man day at subsidized price. The Central committee had approved 320 projects at an estimated cost of over Rs 906 crores for the Sixth plan period. During the years 1985–86, an amount of Rs 400 crores was allotted for the implementation of NERP. The Seventh plan envisaged providing employment to the unemployed generation. According to outlays during the first three years of the Seventh plan for both the programmes were stepped up and placed around Rs 1200 crores per annum, which generated about 600 millions man days of employment each year.[49]

Both the NREP and RLEGP could hardly achieve the desired goal. Hence, the finance minister of India in his budget speech in 1990 announced a new scheme for intensive employment to be implemented in 120 backward districts with an outlay of Rs 500 crores. It was this scheme which came to be known as the Jawahar Rozgar Yojana (JRY). It was all done at the initiative of the then Prime Minister Rajiv Gandhi. Under the JRY the expenditure was to be shared between the Centre and the states on 80:20 ratio. It was also decided to release the Central share directly to the concerned districts which was to be utilized by the Village Panchayats. The NREP and the RLEGP were merged into the

JRY. The main objective of the JRY was to "provide fuller employment opportunities to at least one member of each family living below the poverty line." It was expected that distribution of resources to Village Panchayats "will result in increasing the coverage to all the rural areas and also ensure the fuller participation of the people in its implementation."[50] The area of the works which were included under the JRY is vast covering all aspects of rural life.

Before launching of the JRY only 65 per cent of villages had been benefited by the rural development programmes. Now it intended to "reach out to every corner of the country and to 440 lac families in rural India living below the poverty line." The government of India provided Rs 2100 crores only in the year 1989–90. Moreover, launching of this Yojana increased both the value and responsibilities of the Village Panchayats because all the plans were to be chalked out by the villagers.[51]

The JRY became very popular all over the country and benefited a number of the rural poor. By providing part-time jobs to the rural poor, it gave them economic relief. Moreover, the construction of village approach roads, village streets, drainage, sheds, community halls, repair of old roads and living accommodations for the poor under the Indira Awas Yojana (IAY) began to change the rural face. It aroused new hopes and aspirations among the rural people. However, keeping in view the larger number of the rural unemployed people and their pathetic economic conditions, the JRY and IAY did hardly meet their requirements. Moreover, the mass illiteracy of the rural poor and mounting corruption among the authorities involved in the affairs, remained big hurdles on the path of poverty alleviation programmes. So the JRY and IAY like other rural development programmes did not cut much ice to eradicate poverty and make the rural poor self-reliant. In spirit, the JRY carried many attributes, but on the ground its performances remained unsatisfactory due to various factors which will be discussed in the succeeding chapter.

Rural Development Schemes in Recent Years

To help the poor and alleviate poverty from the country has been the popular slogan of the political parties and various governments since seventies of the last century. With the passage of years, the government of India went on changing the plans for rural development one after the other. The SFDA, MFAL, DPAA, HADP, TADPCSRD, FFW programmes were not directly related to rural people living below the poverty line. Moreover, these programmes instead of removing poverty rather increased gap between the rich and the poor because of mismanagement of funds by the vested interests. Both the government servants and various agencies availed the opportunity to enrich themselves deceiving the real beneficiaries.

The National Democratic Alliance led by the Bhartiya Janata Party (BJP) under the prime ministership of Atal Behari Vajpayee, launched another rural development programme in April 1999. This programme called as Swaranjayanti Gram Swarozgar Yojana (SGSY) replaced the earlier self-employment and allied programmes running under the JRY. The SGSY aimed at "establishing large number of micro-enterprises in the rural areas" offering "perfect balance of credit and subsidy."[52] Among the Swarozgarists at least 55 per cent must be the members of the scheduled castes and scheduled women and 3 per cent disabled. Thereafter, the NDA government launched another Yojana, namely, Samagra Awas Yojana (SAY) with a purpose "to improve the quality of life of people and over all habitats in the rural areas." Another Yojana, namely, Jawahar Gram Samridhi Yojana (JGSY) also came into being for "creation of demand driven community village infrastructure including durable assets at the village level and assets to enable the rural poor to increase the opportunities for employment" and also for "generation of supplementary employment for the unemployed poor in the rural areas."[53]

Thereafter, when the Indian National Congress formed the government under the leadership of Manmohan Singh, it championed the cause of the poor and adopted schemes and programmes to eradicate poverty from the nation. The government of Manmohan Singh launched a scheme, namely, National Rural Guaranteed Employment Programme (NREGP) with the objective to provide guaranteed employment at least for 100 days in a year to the people living below the line of poverty. It opened wide scope for employment in the rural areas all over the nation. The central government directed all state governments to launch such schemes and help the poor to upgrade their living standard. The government sanctioned enough money to provide ways to the rural employees under NREGP. The purpose of the NREGP is not only to provide employment to the deserving rural people but also to change the rural face by constructing link roads, approach roads, tanks, sheds, water saviors etc. Besides that the government adopted the scheme to provide foodgrains on monthly basis to the backward, deprived, suppressed and neglected families at the cheapest rate by issuing Red and Green Cards. Such bold and dynamic steps of the Congress government during the regime of Manmohan Singh, in fact, provided enough job opportunity to the rural workers at their home. It helped migration of the labourers to the urban areas in search of jobs.

Analysis of Rural Development Programmes

A general survey and review of various rural development programmes launched in India during the regime of different governments, reveals the fact that the Government of India has the wish to help the poor and improve their economic conditions, but lack the will and spirit to implement the programmes with full determination and required commitment. The government went on changing the plans and schemes from time to time for rural development one after another in search of better avenues, but without doing required homework. The programmes such as SFDA, MFAL, DPAA, HADP, TADPCSRD, FFW etc, were not directly related to the rural people living below the line of poverty. Moreover, these programmes instead of removing poverty rather increased gap between the rich and the poor for rural development before the application of IRDP. When these programmes were launched, the suppressed and deprived sections of the people were yet far from the eyes of the government. Some marginal farmers did avail the opportunity to get benefits from such programmes, but the big farmers intervened and succeeded in pocketing most of the benefits.

Secondly, the government did not remain firm to the decision regarding rural development schemes. The government lost enough time for making experiment in rural development. It reveals the truth that the government was not satisfied with the schemes. That is why it frequently changed them. Different governments launched different schemes just to earn a reputation in the field of rural development. Thirdly, the government instead of mentally preparing the people for participating in plans formulation and their implementation, did little to ensure their full implementation with the result that socially, economically and educationally backward rural people could hardly avail the opportunities to get actual benefits of the development schemes and projects . Rather, "the discretionary power exercised by different categories of government officials opened up "scope for harassment, malpractices and corruption." It is true that such programmes benefited numbers of poor families and helped in changing the ugly rural face, but the targets fixed have not yet been achieved. SN Misra and K Sharma are of the view that "with a view to forestalling the dangers of bureaucratic elitism and the totalitarianism, people's participation becomes imperative." [54]

In the case of India, bureaucrats and government officials attached to the rural development programme hardly remained committed and true to the spirit needed for success of the programmes. Various studies in this field made by different agencies and institutions reveal the truth that the major benefits of rural development have been pocketed by economically better off, socially high-up in social stratification and politically advanced sections of the rural communities.[55] Even the Planning Commission of India accepted the truth that "Much of the benefits from infrastructure have accrued largely to the relatively affluent ... Many segments of population like scheduled castes and scheduled tribes have not shared fully in the benefit growth."[56] The study reveals that the Panchayati Raj Institutions have always been under the domination of economically and socially privileged sections of rural society.

With the expanding infrastructural and administrative scope of development administration, which brought various new set of rules and regulations increasing discretionary powers of the government officials opened new avenues for corruption and bribery. Rising corruption and bribery created the myth among the people that nothing could be done until the government servants related to the affairs are bribed. Under such corrupt circumstance neither the CDP nor the IRDP, JRY and other schemes could do much to remove poverty from the country. The subordinate officers delegated with power began to delay the required actions knowingly just for receiving bribes from the parties concerned. The political leaders instead of correcting and controlling the corrupt officials provided political patronage to them with the result that corruption became an established order of the day;[57] all anti-corruption drives have failed to control corruption and check the declining moral standard of the government officials.

Thus, it is obvious that despite numerous programmes and projects with the marked objectives to improve the living standard, the millions of rural people living below the line of poverty the results, which have come out, are not only discouraging but disappointing too. Chandrika Singh firmly believes that the benefits coming out of the development programmes go either to the government servants....or to the brokers (dalals) who are in the front of the que to usurp the benefits meant for poor sections, especially Harijans and Adivasis. The poor, backward and illiterate people could not even understand the procedures of obtaining credit facilities for self-employment. The behaviour of the dealing authorities was so much rough and harsh that the rural backward people dared not question the so-called public servants."[58]

The government of India provided crores of rupees to alleviate poverty. It is true that vocational training institutes in the fields of carpentry, driving, knitting and embroidery, welding, soldering etc. were opened, but on papers to obtain money and line their own pockets. Stipends were admitted, but that also in the paper with the objective to receive the stipend money by the proprietor. Those who are really admitted are never paid the full amount. Under the scheme of essential supplies through the fair price shops, Mukhiyas or Pradhans, BDOs, COs, and personnel of supply departments—they formed a nexus to plunder the government money. The cooperative credit societies and rural banks are full of problems. They are serving the needs of those who are rich and crooked.

Thus, even after half a century of India's independence the picture of the rural India and the conditions of the poor living in the slum areas of big cities and towns, is not satisfactory. There are millions of people who are sunk into acute poverty and scarcity. Millions are yet jobless. Their dirty economic conditions and insecure dark and dirty gloomy future have not only caused worries to them but also have dampened their spirit. They are loitering hither and thither in search of jobs. On the other hand, a handful of beneficiaries are enjoying luxurious lives at the cost of the poor. The process of development in the rural sections, in the words of Dandekar and Nilkantha "has benefited the upper middle and richer sections much more than the middle, the lower middle and the poorer sections."[59] The picture in the urban areas also is the same. Regarding the shabby condition of the poor living in the urban areas, Dandekar and Nilkantha writes that "the lower middle and poor sections constituting the lowest 40 per cent of the urban population have not benefited at all by the economic development.[60]

Despite all this, the government deserves full appreciation for its concern and efforts to think about poverty alleviation programme and their implementation under the administrative administration. It is the government's efforts, which have brought millions of the poor in action sharpening their consciousness. Millions of the poor have been provided houses under the scheme of Indira Awas Yojana. Millions of manual workers have received economic relief under the running development schemes. The government must be appreciated for diverting government funds towards the development of the rural areas. Many villages have been linked with the main roads, which have decreased the troubles and inconveniences of the people. If corruption is checked in time, there is no doubt, the schemes and programmes running under the development administration would definitely reduce the poverty in the country and change the ugly rural face. India is a vast country where majority of the people are poor and their living conditions are vulnerable. There is too much scarcity of jobs. The Indian labourers are hard-working lot but they need avenues of jobs. The part-time jobs which have been provided to them under various development schemes are not sufficient. Until permanent jobs are provided to them, it is impossible to eradicate poverty from the country. The growing population of the country especially among the poor Indians is another big hurdle to improve their economic conditions. No doubt, the country is rich in its natural resources, but it needs proper exploitation with sincere efforts. The country has the expertise, but not proper planning. What is needed at the movement is sincerity of the government and efforts of the people to change the socio-economic structure of the country. There is no dearth of scheme and plans for development in India. What the country and people need immediately are the honest administrators, and ministers who have job knowledge. There is also the need to arouse feeling and enthusiasm among the people to take part actively in development administration at grassroots level all over the country.

Endnotes

1. P.N. Singh, "Rural Development: Some Basic Issues", in Devendra K. Das (Ed), *Indian Economy after 50 years of Independence: Experience and challenges.* Deep and Deep Publications, New Delhi, 1998, p. 9.
2. Ibid.
3. Ganguly, B.N & Gupta D.B., (1976), *Levels of Living in India,* New Delhi, pp. 233–34.

4. Desai A.R., (1966), *Social Background and Indian Socialism,* Bombay, pp. 182–83.

5. Tara Chand (1967*), The History of the Freedom Movement of India*, Vol. II, New Delhi, pp. 279-80.

6. Chaudhary Shukhbir (1971), *Peasants' and Workers' Movement in India* (1905–1929), Delhi, p. 7.

7. Singh Chandrika (1986), *Socialism in India: Rise, Growth and Prospects*, B.R. Publishing Corporation New Delhi, p. 39.

8. Pattabhi Sitaramaya (1969), *The History of Indian National Congress (1885–1935),* Vol. I, Delhi, p. 343.

9. Ibid. Also see, *Report of the 45th Indian National Congress, Karachi*, 1931, p. 109

10. Chakravorty, S., (1985*),* *Development Planning: The Indian Experience*, Clarendon Press Oxford, p. 10.

11. Nehru's Message- Summary Record of Annual Conferences on Community Development held at Mount Abu, Published by the Ministry of Community Development Government of India, New Delhi, 1950, p. 13.

12. Inamdar, N.R. (1992), *Development Administration in India,* New Delhi, p. 21.

13. *Community Development, Panchayati Raj and Cooperative,* Publication Division, Government of India, New Delhi, 1964, p. 6.

14. *Report of the Team for the Study of the Community Project and National Extension Service,* Vol. One, New Delhi, 1956-57, p. 1.

15. Inamdar, N.R. (1992), *Development Administration in India*, op. cit. p. 15.

16. Misra, B.B. (1986) *Government and Bureaucracy in India,* Oxford Publications, New Delhi, p. 352.

17. Ibid. p. 351.

18. *Seventh Evaluation Report on Community Development and Allied Fields, Programme Evaluation Organisation, Planning Commission*, New Delhi, 1960. pp. 121-36.

19. *Report of the Team for the Study of the Community Project and National Extension Service*, New Delhi, Vol. One, New Delhi, November, 1957, p. 5.

20. Ibid. Para 22-8, p. 7.

21. Ibid.

22. Inamdar, N.R., (1961), Report of the Study of Administration of Community Project, Block Haveli, University of Poona, pp. 19-25.
23. Inamdar, N.R. (1992), *Development Administration in India,* op. cit., p. 73.
24. Ibid. p. 76.
25. Misra, B.B. *District Administration and Rural Development*, op. cit., p. 331.
26. *Report of the Team for the Study of the Community Project and National Extension Service*, New Delhi, Vol. One, New Delhi, November, p. 3.
27. Jaques, S (1977), *A New Reflection in Participation in Developed and Developing Countries,* Vol. II, Delhi, p. 110.
28. Misra, S.N (1992), "People's Participation in Rural Development Programme", Mohinder Singh (Ed), *Rural Development in India: Current Perspective,* New Delhi, p. 126.
29. Ibid.
30. Planning Commission, Five Year Plan (1969–1974), Government of India, New Delhi, p. 2.
31. Ali Sadiq, *Indian National Congress: Resolution on Economic Policy, Programme and Allied Matter,* 1924-1968, Delhi, p. 146.
32. Planning Commission, Fourth Five Year Plan, Govt. of India op. cit. pp. 2-3.
33. Misra, B.B. *District Administration and Rural Development*, op. cit., p. 331.
34. Reddy Ram, "Panchayati Raj Proposals", a paper presented in the seminar held at New Delhi, No. 234, February, 1979, pp. 1-37.
35. Report on the Panchayati Raj Institution Chapter VI (Planning), Govt. of India, New Delhi, 1978,.
36. *Ganguly's Studies in Indian Economic Problem, Calcutta,* 1980, p. 700.
37. Maithani, B.B., "Organizational Design for Rural Development in North East India", in Phukon Girin (Ed) 1989, *Dynamics of Development Administration in North East India,* Delhi, p. 49
38. Verma B.M and Singh D.P., (1991), *IRDP,* New Delhi, p. 31.
39. Misra S.N. and Verma B. P., (1979), "Evaluation of Training of Rural Youth for Self-Employment in Rajasthan", *Indian Institute of Public Administration*, New Delhi, p. 79.

40. Verma B.M and Singh D.P., (1991), *IRDP*, New Delhi, p. 31.

41. Radha Raman Singh and Narayan N., "IRDP and Revitalization of Rural Schemes in India", *Khadi Gramodyog,* Vol. XXXI, No. 4, January 1985, Bombay, p. 177.

42. Sixth five Year Plan (1980-85), Planning Commission, Government of India, New Delhi, p. 32.

43. *Gramin Vikas News Letter*, Vol. 1, No. 2, November, 1985, published by the Department of Rural Development, Government of India, New Delhi, pp. 2-3.

44. Ibid. Vol. II, February, 1986, p.2.

45. Sharma S.K. and Malhotra S. L., (1977), *Integrated Rural Development Approach Strategy and Perspective*, New Delhi, p. 77.

46. *Guidelines of Rural Industries, Components of IRDO/TRYSEM* in Government of India, Ministry of Rural Reconstruction December, 11979.

47. *Gramin Vikas News Letter*, Vol. 5, No. 8-9, August –September, 1987, op. cit. p. 18.

48. *TRYSEM,* a hand book, published by the Government of India, Ministry of Rural Development, New Delhi, 1980.

49. *Gramin Vikas News Letter*, Vol. 1, No. 2, November, 1985, published by the Department of Rural Development, Government of India, New Delhi, pp. 6-7..

50. *Jawahar Rojgar Yojna* (JRY), a manual, published by the Government of India, Ministry of Agriculture, New Delhi, August 1989.

51. *Gramin Vikas News Letter,* Vol. 5, No. 8-9, August –September, 1987, op. cit. p. 19.

52. *SGSY,* a booklet, issued by the Government of India, Ministry of Rural Development, New Delhi, 1999. p 1.

53. Ibid.

54. Sharma S.N. and Mishra K., "Insuring People's Participation in Rural Development Programme", op. cit., p. 6.

55. Shastri Sriniwas, "Pattern of Panchayati Raj", *Indian Journal of Public Administration*, vol. VIII, No. 4, October-December, 1962, p. 460.

56. Roy, T.K., "Some Though on Community Participation", *Kurukshetra,* Vol. XXXI, May 116-21, 1983, p. 18.

57. Dandekar V.M and Rath Nilkantha (1991), *Poverty in India*, Bombay, p. 28.
58. Singh Chandrika, *Socialism in India*, op. cit. pp. 194-95.
59. The Report of the Rural Urban Committee, Government of India New Delhi,1966, 1966, pp. 311—32.
60. Ibid. p. 30.

Chapter – 5

Achievement and Failure of Centrally Sponsored Schemes for Rural Development

As discussed in the succeeding chapter, the Government of India especially under the leadership of Mrs. Indira Gandhi and Rajiv Gandhi was fully determined to change the economic shape of the rural areas and provide enough scope for economic development of the people living below the poverty line. Hence, the government directed the Planning Commission to include the rural development schemes and programmes in the Five-Year Plans and provide sufficient financial help to implement such programmes. Hence, all the district collectors, district magistrates were directed to take keen interest in implementation of such schemes and programme to improve the living standard of millions of the poor rural people. Special instructions were issued to the authorities of District Rural Development Agency (DRDA) to work in this regard with the development blocks of the district without delay.

Putting emphasis on full implementation of the plan outlays and target, the deputy chairman of the Planning Commission wrote D.O. Letter to the chief ministers of the states, and union territories that "All out efforts need to be mounted to implement the plan fully and effectively". The letter further stated that "The Prime Minister is... very keen about effective implementation and monitoring of our plan."[1] Thereafter, the Seventh Plan adopted some more vigorous steps to gear up the rural economy and help the poor masses.

Industry Service and Business (ISB) and TRYSEM

Since the IRDP was committed to eradicate poverty from rural India by making marked development in production and providing employment to rural masses, the Government of India thought of creating two components of the IRDP which are the Industry Service and Business (ISB) and the Training of Rural Youth for Self-Employment (TRYSEM). The former scheme was initiated through a government circular dated 20 February 1979 and the latter through another circular dated 20 July 1979. The circular concerning the ISB addressed to concerned authority of the states, puts emphasis on promotion and development of rural industries and rural artisan programme under IRDP in 2000 blocks under DPAP/SFDA/CADP and also in blocks under the Area Planning Schemes for full employment.[2] The circular further stated that the Government of India had approved the inclusion of Rural Industries Programme (RIP) and Rural Artisan Programme (RAP) for implementation in 2000 blocks. So it could be the main duty or the district industries centre (DICs) to promote and develop cottage, small scales and tiny industries and small industries and services in the rural areas. They were asked to utilize the available funds provided under the IRDP for the promotion of industries and other programmes. The DICs were also instructed to make an assessment of the potentialities of the rural industries by making use of available data in various respects. They were asked to identify and specify the industries/enterprises fit for promotion and development in each block and provide financial as well as material assistance to the identified participants to enable them to set up the units chosen by them. The circular stated, "It is considered very necessary that full advantage

Table-I

Central Plan Outlay for Major Schemes of Social Sector and Rural Development (Rs in crores)

Ministry/Department	1990--91 BE BE	1995--96 BE RE	1996-97 BE RE	1997-98 BE RE
Education (General)	856 - 837	1828- 2504	3388- 2574	4095-3350
Education (Elementary)	N A	265 - 224	651- 1443	2264- 1567
Education (Adult)	94 - 96	131 - 234	170 - 225	112 - 127
Health Education	275 - 255	670 - 649	815 - 818	995 - 918
Family welfare	675 - 785	1581- 1506	1535- 1547	1829-1828
Women/ Child	228 - 255	588 - 679	682 - 682	734 - 600
Welfare	364 - 366	890 - 890	890 - 890	1389 - 804
Rural Development	3130-2975	7700-8284	8632-7775	9001-8290
JRY Employment	1935-2095	2100-2101	3862-2955	1865-1655
Rural Artisans	377-356	656- 656	656-646 -	611-532
Water Supply/Sanitation	443 - 421	1170	1170-1115	1402-1402
Indira Awas Yojna	N A	NA 492	1194-1194	1190-1144
Millions Wells Schemes	NA	211	448 - 388	448 - 373
Nehru Rozgar Yojana	1220 -110	71 - 68	71 - 50	80 - 31
Self Employment for Industrial unemployed Youths	37 - 53	-- --	-- --	--- --
PM Rozgar Yojana	NA	145 - 145	145 - 115	145 - 95
SJSRY	--- ---	---- ----	----- ---	---- 103.
Total Plan Expenditure	5816-5694	13612-14831	16323-14616	18394-16446

Source- Budget Reports

should be taken of these provisions for training under the IRDP and training may be imparted in Indian Technological Institutes, polytechnic, training schools run by the Khadi and Village Industry Corporation".

The Indira Awas Yojana (IAY) and the Million Wells Scheme (MWS) were earlier the sub-schemes of JRY. From 1 January 1995, they have become separate schemes. It was integrated with

Table-II

PROGRESS ON TRYESM

Period Plan	No of Youths to be trained.	No of Youths trained	No of Youths self-employed	No of Youth employed	Total
Sixth Plan	1009440	114695	48396	102097	580493
Seventh Plan	N. A.	997960	464036	131096	595123
1990-91	425314	236177	123785	41493	165278
1991-92	425314	307004	199959	47459	167418
1992-93	300000	275993	99334	42058	141392
1993-94	350000	304000	107519	42711	150230
1994-95	322331	106000	31979	7635	49614
Grand total	2832389	3203304	1425008	414549	1839557

PMRY—a rationalized version of the erstwhile schemes of Urban Basis Services. NRY and PM's Yojana Integrated Urban Poverty.

Table - II indicates that the progress on TRYSEM scheme is not satisfactory, as the years rolled down the rural youths began to take little interest in the programme with the result that the number employed under such scheme began to fall. During Sixth Five-Year Plan 1,014,695 youths were trained while only 580,493 youths were employed. During Seventh Five-Year Plan, 595,132 youths were employed. From eighth plan onwards the number of employed under TRYSEM scheme began to decline, to 39,614 youths up to November 1994.

The number of trained youths was greater for instance in 1992–94—275,993 youths were trained. During 1993–94, 364,000 youths were trained. It shows that the avenues for employment of the youths under TRYSEM scheme were not up to mark and congenial.

It further stated that after completion of training, the trainees may be given assistance up to a maximum of Rs. 5000/- by way of loan from a bank and this may be subsidized to the tune of 33½ per cent subject to a maximum of Rs. 1500/-. Instruction was also given to choose at least 100 families in each block every year for the industries and artisan activities. The identified beneficiaries under rural industries programme were to be given financial assistance for buying tools and equipments.

The training of rural youth for self-employment programme, too, put emphasis on removing poverty from the rural society. It covered, in addition to other persons below the poverty line, the people who were poor but not below the poverty line. The purpose was to protect them from falling below the line of poverty. It concentrated especially on the youth. Training preference was given to those who were below the age of 35 years. Moreover, those youths were accepted for obtaining technical training that did not possess any technical skill. Here assistance is still given to those who have regained technical training under the provision, but in case of IRDP persons are identified for assistance even without training. The basic aim of the IRDP and TRYSEM was to diversify the rural people to the non-agriculture sector so that the burden on the sector could be reduced and rural workers might avail some extra opportunities of employment. This had been initiated with a sole motive to provide skill and training to rural youths so that after getting skill and infrastructural facilities they may embark upon a career of self-employment. The Central government decided, in the beginning, to extend the activities of the IRDP in 5011 blocks of the country with active involvement of officials, common masses, community leader and business houses.

The training of the rural youth for self-employment programme was basically a rural programme and its basic aim was to develop human resource potential in the rural areas.[3] This was an attempt to create a more broad-based training system suited to the needs of rural India. It was more informal and flexible training system with less emphasis on paper qualification and other rules, and was considered to be better tuned to the long run requirement of the economy.[4] There was proposal to train about 200000 rural youths in the country every year in various skills. Under this scheme during the year 1979–80 and 1980–81, 93,018 rural youths were trained in various skills and trades like tailoring, electrical fittings, Kashidakari (embroidery), welding, carpet making, cycle repairing etc. According to the governmental report out of that 9276 youths had already become self-employed.

An important component of the TRYSEM scheme was its provision for strengthening of existing training infrastructure such as construction of hostels and dormitories, classrooms and workshop accommodation, training equipment and aids etc. The government sanctioned a good deal of amount for this purpose;[6] it is interesting to note that numerous rural youths have got the opportunities for obtaining training. Many of them have obtained self-employment also. But there were still crores of rural youths who remain deprived of such facilities either due to their ignorance or due to the authorities' non-accessibility.

The District Rural Development Agency (DRDA) was made fully responsible for controlling and guiding the rural development activities. Blocks were adopted as the basic units of planning and implementation of various programmes. Special staff was recruited to give practical shape to the policies in regard to change the economic face of rural India.

In the early stage under the ISB there was target of one hundred beneficiaries per block per year. Now the target has been raised to the six hundred beneficiaries (families) under each block per year. Under TRYESM, in the beginning, the government had decided to train hundred youths per block per year. Now there is increase in this programme, too. This limit has been relaxed and any number of youths eager to acquire skill can be selected for training. The cost of training is borne both by the central and state governments on 5:50 basis.

Problems of Declination in Implementation of Programmes

It is very clear that the governments of late Mrs. Indira Gandhi and Rajiv Gandhi were deeply interested in rural development. The government took up maximum possible schemes and plans to improve the economic lot of the rural poor. Both the ISB and the TRYESM programmes were meant for those families which were sunk in poverty either due to lack of employment opportunities or want of technical skills. However, the vital problem before the government was how to implement such programmes effectively, especially selection of the beneficiaries. There were many vested interests that were always active and devious enough to usurp the benefits of the programmes. There was attraction for credit facilities on cheap rate and subsidy on the credit which attracted the wealthy persons to take undue advantage of the provisions. AK Pandey has rightly observed, "The families below the poverty line will have to be listed under different income groups starting from the lowest ... priority in selection will have to be accorded to the poorest of the families... but selection of the beneficiaries was in the hand of the concerned staff of the blocks who hardly remained sincere while performing their duties".[7]

Second problem was selection of the fields for industries in the rural areas. The type of industries should be fruitful with a scope for more production and markets for sale of the produced goods. There should also be scope for gainful employment. The participants should have been given required equipments, skill, guidance, inputs, etc. It had been observed that there were several participants who came ahead for installing industries neither for employment nor for production, but for obtaining loan from the banks or from the concerned agencies expecting the gain of subsidies. The government had, in fact, observed such temptation of the vested interests. The government had suggested that while selecting areas for installation of industries in the rural areas, the scope for employment and markets for sales must be kept in mind. So the government had emphasized on need for adequate and proper planning of industrial development in the rural areas. But reality is that the directions of the government were not heeded while implementing the programmes.

There was emphasis on the fact that the data should be collected from the village level by using the village level workers. Further, in order to identify industries and enterprises fit for promotion and development in each block, the accent would have to be on the assessment of local demands and resources. The guidelines provided by the ministry of rural reconstruction mentioned that agencies which provided a package of services to a single industry or a group of related industries were more successful than multi-product organisation. Therefore, the focus should have been on setting up or strengthening of such cooperatives, corporations or boards at the state and district level. The guidelines also suggested setting up rural marketing and service centers of village industry and marketing organizations. These should have been serving agencies. The rural marketing and serving centers could be set up by state level board and corporations through the all-India bodies in the decentralized sector.

According to the report of the Council for Advancement of People's Action and Rural Technology, one of the weaknesses of the IRDP has been weak marketing strategy and inadequate linkage for the products of the beneficiaries of anti-poverty programmes.[8] Keeping in view the aforesaid facts, a marketing division was set up to be manned by experts. Its basic function was to draw up strategy on marketing and creation of linkages between groups of rural producers and marketing outlets. The division would provide consultancy and advice not only to voluntary organizations but also to various other IRDP groups set up through district rural development agencies.[9]

The Council for Advancement of People's Action and Rural Technology has sanctioned thousands of schemes. In 1988–89 alone it sanctioned 1072 projects involving a total assistance of Rs. 82.02 corers. In the previous years, the corresponding figures were 549 and Rs. 12.68 crores. The projects sanctioned by the Council covered various steps of the rural life such as sericulture, dairy development, village industries, minor irrigation, fodder production and certain social activities.[10]

Programmes for Rural Landless and Unemployed People

The direct attack on eradication of poverty from the rural areas consists of two strategies. Firstly, self-employment schemes and secondly, the wage employment programmes of the National Rural

Employment Programme and Rural Landless Employment Guarantee Programme (NREGP). The NREGP came into being in October, 1980 and the RLEGP in 1983. The aim of NREGP was to provide supplementary employment to the unemployed and underemployed for the rural masses, generating assets and improving the nutritional level of the poor in the rural areas. The RLEGP was introduced with the similar objectives. A specific feature of this programme as distinct from NREGP was that it was expected to provide guaranteed employment for a minimum period of 100 days in a year to one member of the landless labour household in the rural areas.

During the Sixth Plan period, these two programmes provided employment of 2034.52 million man-days with an outlay of Rs. 2,750 crores. Despite this macro-level achievement, the Sixth Plan ended with light backlog of unemployment in the rural fields. For the year 1985–86 an employment target of 228 millions man-days was fixed. The half yearly target up to September 1985 was 82 million man-days, which corresponded to 36 per cent of the annual target. The reported employment generation up to September 1985 stood at over 92 million man-days, which accounted for over 40 per cent of the annual target and exceeded the half yearly target by 12.3 per cent. Out of the total employment of over 92 millions man-days, employment generated for scheduled castes and scheduled tribes are 32 million and 15 million man-days respectively. Allocation of Rs. 230 crores was made as a central assistance under NREP for the year 1985–86. A quantity of 2.3 lac mts of foodgrain was also allotted for distribution among the workers at the rate of one kilogram per man-day at subsidized prices. About half lac tons of foodgrain was utilized.

The central committee had approved 320 projects at an estimated cost of over Rs. 906 crores for the Sixth Plan period. During the year 1985–86 an amount of Rs. 400 crores was allocated for the programme.[11] The Seventh Five-Year Plan envisaged providing employment to all the unemployed in the rural areas. About 45 per cent of the employment generation was expected from the investments in the agricultural sector and the rest from the specific programme of NREP and RLEGP. According to outlays, during the first three years of the Seventh Plan for both the programmes were stepped up and placed around Rs. 1200 crores per annum, which generated about 600 millions man-days of employment each year.

Poverty Alleviation Programmes Assessment

A general survey of the programmes and their implementation under the IRDP and the NREP/RLEGP reveals the truth that the government took up decisive steps to eradicate poverty from the rural areas and provide economic relief to the people concerned. The major thrust was on provision for employment. It is true that these programmes provided economic relief to the poor sections of the people to a considerable extent. But reality is that the result which was expected could hardly be achieved. The corruption prevailed from top to bottom in the development blocks and the ignorance of the rural people was vital factor responsible for slow progress. Moreover, the rapidly growing population especially among the poor sections of the people who lacked the knowledge and tectonic of birth control, was also responsible for blocking the way of removing poverty from the rural areas. However, these programmes generated new hope among the poor people and encouraged them to fight against poverty with the help of the government's financial and technical assistance.

Jawahar Rozgar Yojana (JRY)

Like the Sixth Plan the Seventh Plan also aimed at reducing the number of unemployment in the rural areas through creating new avenues of employment. The plan was made to provide employment in each rural family. The finance minister in his budget speech of the year 1989–90 announced a new scheme, namely, the Jawahar Rozgar Yojana (JRY) for intensive employment in backward districts to be implemented in 120 districts. Provision for Rs. 500 crores was made. It was done at the initiative of the then Prime Minister Rajiv Gandhi.

The JRY is popular scheme for the rural upliftment. Under the scheme, the expenditure is shared between the centre and the states at the 80:20 ratios. Secondly, there is provision to release the central share directly to the districts. Further, not less than 80 per cent of the allocation under the programme received by the districts is required to be given to the village Panchayats. The NREP and RLEGP were merged in the newly launched RJY with the result that it comprises all the schemes running under the NREP and RLGEP. The objective of the JRY is to "Provide fuller employment opportunities to at least one member of each family living under the poverty line who seeks unskilled employment." It has been hoped that "distribution of resources to all the rural areas and also ensure the fuller participation of the people in its implementation."[12]

Table-III

Physical and Financial Progress under Jawahar Rozgar Yojana and the Employment Assurance scheme

Period	Allocation (Rs. in crores)	Utilization	Employment Target (lakh)	Employment done (Lakh)
1989-90	2360.67	2458.11	875.7	864.4
1990-91	2627.80	2588.52	929.1	874.6
1991-92	2620.90	2659.89	735.4	808.1
1992-93	3169.05	2704.76	753.8	782.1
1993-94 (1st stream)	3181.22	3580.82	1038.3	950.2
1993-94 2nd Stream)	878.20	216.91	------	55.6
1994-95 1st stream	3498.72	3359.59	799.7	745.3
1994-95 2nd stream	878.20	908.45	186.8	206.3

Source: Ministry of Rural Development, Monthly Progress Report/Annual Report, Various Issues.

JRY is more interested in providing employment to those poor masses that totally depend on physical labour for their livelihood. There are various fields of workers in the rural areas, which require immediate improvement. The following is the list of works which have been brought under the JRY.

1. Social forestry works on government and community lands belonging to Panchayats etc, road side plantation along canal banks or on waster lands, on sides of railways lines, involving planning of fuel, fodder and fruit trees, distribution of sapling for plantation on private lands, provide the sale proceeds.
2. Soil and water conservation works, water harvesting structure.
3. Minor irrigation works such as construction of community irrigation wells, construction of intermediary and main drains and field channels etc and their improvements.
4. Flood protection, drainage and water logging works.
5. Construction/renovation of village tanks for providing water for human use of cattle or for irrigation.
6. Irrigation wells and field channels on individual holdings of members SC/ST and allotment of ceiling surplus land, *bhoodan* land and government land.
7. Construction of institutional sanitary latrines in rural areas and institutional rural sanitation work like drains soaker pits near handpump stand posts on community/institution basis.
8. Construction of houses for individual member of SC/ST and freed bonded labourers.
9. Construction of rural roads subject to prescribed standards and specifications in accordance with the MNP criteria.
10. Land development and reclamation of wasteland or degraded land with special emphasis on ecological improvement in hill and desert areas.
11. Augmentation of existing ground water resource through micro-level ecological planning involving forestation, soil moisture conservation and water management.
12. Construction of rural bank buildings, godowns for storage or inputs, community work sheds for target group beneficiaries, community centre, Panchayati *ghars* (house), market yards etc.

13. Works of a purely social and community nature such as dispensaries, community centers, anganwadis etc.

14. The primary school buildings.

Thus, it is obvious that the working scope of the JRY is very large. It touches all the aspects of the rural construction. These works provide supplementary employment to the rural labourers and meant for village development. It also aims to improve the overall quality of life in the villages.[13]

Period	Allocation Generation[b]	Person days of employment generation In lacs
1989–90	20,960	864.4
1990–91	20,010 (“4.5)	874.7 (1.2)
1991–92	18,252 (“8.7)	808.1 (“7.6)
1992–93	25,462 (39.5)	778.3 (“2.5)
1993–94	33,063 (29.9)	1,023.7 (38.9)
1994–95[a] (up to Nov.)	38,550 (16.6)	470.6

Note : a. Target figures.

b. Figures in brackets are percentage changes.

Source : Planning commission (1994), Report 1994, Govt. of India New Delhi.

Under the JRY 30 per cent jobs are reserved for rural women. Before the introduction of the JRY only a few per cent of the villages had been benefited. But the JRY covers almost all the villages through Panchayats. Each panchayat is given every year a fixed amount in tune of lacs to spend for village development. Village panchayats are supposed to play main role in the development of the villages.[14]

General Survey of JRY

A general survey of the working of the JRY reveals the truth that the funds allotted by both the central and provincial governments are yet insufficient keeping in view the large size of the villages and their population. The number of rural workers is large. It has failed to provide jobs to every member of the poor rural family. Moreover, the jobs which are given through it are not of permanent nature. Secondly, in several states of India the village panchayats are either defunct or inactive with the result that the funds allotted have not been properly utilized. Thirdly, the officials related to the Yojana are neither honest nor committed. There are several cases of mismanagement or malpractices of government funds. The wide corruption prevailed among the officials and also among the people has badly interrupted the progress of the JRY. Fourthly, the illiteracy among the rural people is another hurdle to take real benefit of the Yojana. These people are easily cheated by the vested interests. The rural work needs full time employment, not part-time.

PR Pogrammes for Rural Development Launched by NDA Govt.

Despite the efforts made over the past few decades, rural poverty in India continues to be significant. While the anti-poverty programmes have been strengthened in successive years, and poverty levels have come down from 56.44 per cent to 37.27 per cent in 1993–94, the number of rural poor has more or less remained static and is estimated to be about 244 million persons.[15] Keeping in view such fact the government of the National Democratic Alliance (NDA) headed by Atal Behari Vajpayee adopted some more policies and programmes to provide economic relief to the rural poor and change the rural economic structure. The IRDP was the only self-employment programme. Later, some more associated programmes were launched without much achievement. The Vajpayee government launched a new programme, namely, Swarnjayanti Gram Swarozgar Yojana (SGSY) on 1 April 1999. This is a holistic programme covering all aspects of self-employment such as organization of the poor into self-help groups, training, credit, technology, infrastructure and marketing. This programme is funded by the centre and the states in the ratio of 75: 25. With the emergence of the SGSY the earlier programmes like IRDP, TRYSEM, DWCRA, SITRA, JRY and MWS are no longer in operation.

In April 1999, the government launched the Jawahar Gram Samridhi Yojana (JGSY) which is the restructured, streamlined and comprehensive version of the erstwhile Jawahar Rozgar Yojana. Its basic objective is to improve the quality of life of the rural poor by providing them additional gainful employment. The secondary objective is the generation of supplementary employment for the unemployed poor in the rural areas. Though the villagers of the poor group are the beneficiaries of the Yojana, especial preference is given to the members of the scheduled castes and the scheduled tribes living below the poverty line. This programme is also implemented entirely at the Village Panchayat level. However, the funds are released through the DRDA and Zilla Parishads. This is centrally sponsored scheme on cost sharing basis between the centre and the states in the ratio of 75: 25.

Keeping in view the requirement of housing, the Indira Awas Yojana (IAY) was started in January 1996. The objective of this Yojana was to help construction of dwelling units and upgradation of existing unserviceable *kucha* houses of members of the scheduled castes and the scheduled tribes. The benefit of this Yojana was extended to widows or next of kin of defense personnel killed in action. The benefit was also extended to ex-service men and retired members of the paramilitary forces as long as they fulfilled the normal eligibility conditions of Indira Awas Yojana.

The SGSY aims at "establishing a large number of micro enterprises in the rural areas, building upon the potential of the rural poor".[16] A significant aspect of the SGSY is that every family assisted under this programme will be brought above the poverty line in three years and therefore the programme aims at "creating substantial additional income for the rural poor".[17] The programme has been designed "to provide proper support and encouragement to tap the inherent talents and capabilities of the rural poor. It will target the most vulnerable among them. At least 50 per cent of the Swarozgarist will be scheduled castes and the scheduled tribes , 40 per cent women and 3 per cent disabled."[18]

This programme focuses on group approach where it involves organisation of the poor into self-help groups. It is also a credit-cum-subsidy programme. The participants are provided loans with subsidies. It stands to cover 30 per cent of the poor in each block. The programme has the provision for promotion of marketing of the goods produced by the SGSY Swarozgarists. Subsidy under it is uniform at 30 per cent of the project cost, subject to a maximum of Rs. 75000. In respect of scheduled castes and the scheduled tribes, however, these are 50 per cent and Rs. 10000 respectively. This programme is implemented through the DRDA with consultation of the Panchayat Samitis. The process of planning, implementation and monitoring integrates the banks and other financial institutions.[19]

The Indira Awas Yojana has proved to be a popular programme all over the country. Targets have been extended in almost every year since its inception. About 53 lac houses have been constructed from 1989–99 under the scheme which provide better relief to the families.[20] The central allocation for 1999–2000 under the IAY is Rs. 1500 crores with a target of about 12.72 out of this Rs. 1280 crores have been allocated for construction of 8.46 lac new houses and 320 crores for conversion of 4.26 lac unserviceable *kutcha* houses into *pucca/semi-pucca* houses. [21]

IAY is a centrally sponsored scheme funded on cost-sharing basis between the Government of India and the states in the ratio of 75: 25. In the case of union territories, the entire resources under the scheme are provided by the Government of India. This scheme is also implemented through the DRDA. The block machinery is entrusted with the responsibility of ensuring that targets for construction of houses under IAY are achieved. At the village level, the Gram Sabha is responsible for selection of beneficiaries.

Besides IAY, the Smgra Awas Yojana (SAY) has recently been launched by the Central government which is a comprehensive scheme with a view to ensuring integrated provision of shelter, sanitation and drinking water. The basic objective of this Yojana is "to improve the quality of life of the people as well as overall habitat in the rural areas."[22] The scheme specifically aims to provide convergence to activities till now separately undertaken such as construction of houses, sanitation facilities and drinking water schemes and ensures their effective implementation by suitable and sustainable induction of technology.[23] This scheme has not yet been extended all over the country. It operated on one block each of 25 districts in 24 states and one union territory.

Analysis of Centrally Sponsored Schemes

At present several centrally sponsored rural schemes are being implemented in the country: these include Indira Awas Yojana, credit-cum subsidy scheme for setting up rural building centers, Loan based Rural Housing Scheme of HUDCO, Golden Jubilee Rural Housing Scheme of National Housing Bank etc. The purpose of launching these schemes is to change the rural shape and help the poor to avail modern technique and facilities of housing. The Government of India has allotted huge amounts of funds to achieve the targets in this regard. All the agencies concerned to give effect to these schemes have been instructed to work hard and honestly to achieve the decided goals. These schemes are monitored by the ministry of rural development through the state government/district authorities.

It is true that the Government of India with the cooperation and assistance of the state governments has been adopting the policies and launching various schemes for transformation of the rural society. It is also true that huge amount of finance has been provided for implementation of these schemes. But it is sad to note that despite such policies of the government, the result is not satisfactory. There is no denying the fact that the houses constructed under the housing schemes and allotment of these houses among the poor and suppressed sections of the people have helped the number of families to get benefits. But keeping in view the greater number of the people living under the line of poverty, it is not sufficient. There are millions of the poor and backward families who are still homeless or are forced to live in the houses which are not fit for human habitation. Moreover, the buildings constructed under the housing schemes are very small in size and lack sanitation. Numerous cases of maladjustment of funds related to implementation of such programmes have been found out. In the name of the poor families or the families belonging to the scheduled castes and the scheduled tribes, honesty is not maintained. With the connivance of the concerned authorities such benefits have gone to those people who do not deserve such assistance. Various cases of malpractices have been discovered. However, corruption has not yet been checked. Those who are selected for benefits do not get full allotted amount due to unscrupulous government officials.

It has been observed that the people for who these programmes have been launched lack the required information and knowledge to get benefits. As a result, they have to depend upon brokers who never hesitate to cheat them. Moreover, the middlemen establish nexus with the concerned government officials and corrupt them. It does not mean that the high officials of the government are unaware about the prevailing corruption but they do not act against the corrupt which encourages the corrupt to be more corrupt. The illiterate villagers do not know how to complain and where to complain against such corrupt officials. They are satisfied with what amount is given to them. They hardly dare to go against concerned government authority.

Latest Rural Development Programme: NREGS

The National Rural Employment Guarantee Act was notified by the Government of India on 7 September 2005 with the marked objective to provide employment to those rural poor who have no alternative other than to do manual work. It laid emphasis on enhancing security in rural areas by providing at least 100 days of guaranteed wage employment in a financial year to every household whose adult members volunteer to do unskilled manual work. The following are its basic goals:

1. Strong social safety net for the vulnerable groups providing fall-back employment source, when other employment alternatives are scarce or inadequate.
2. Growth engine for sustainable development of an agricultural economy. Through the processor providing employment on works that address causes of chronic poverty such as drought, deforestation and soil erosion the Act seeks to strengthen the natural resource base of rural livelihood and create durable assents in rural areas. Effectively implemented, NREGA has the potential to transform the geography of poverty.
3. Employment of rural poor through the process of a rights-based law.

In the beginning, this Act was notified in 200 districts with effect from 2 February 2006. In the financial year 2007–2008, it was extended to additional 130 districts. From April 2008, all the remaining districts of the country were brought under the umbrella of the NREGA. The Village Panchayat is to play vital role in providing guaranteed employment to the rural poor. Those who need works have to go for registration through the Village Panchayat, which issues a job card after verification. The job card holders are to submit a written application for employment to the Gram Panchayat stating the time and duration for which work is sought. Employment is given within 15 days of application for work. In case employment is not given the job card holder is entitled to get daily employment allowance. Work should be provided within 5 km radius of the village. Wages are to be paid according to piece rate or daily rate, but payment must be made on weekly basis. At least one-third beneficiaries must be women workers. The central government bears the 100 per cent wage cost of unskilled manual labour and 75 per cent of the material cost including the wages of skilled and semi-skilled workers. The expenditure involved is borne by the Gram

Sabha. There is also provision for grievances redressal mechanism to be put in place for ensuring a responsive implementation process. All accounts and records relating to the Scheme should be available for public scrutiny. The Gram Sabha recommends works to be taken up under NREGS. The Village panchayat is pivotal body for implementation at the village level. Where Part Nine of the constitution does not apply, local councils/authorities as mandated by the state concerned are invested with corresponding responsibilities. At the block level the programme officer as the coordinator is responsible for consolidation of plans. He is accountable to the district programmes coordinator.

All the plans in this regard are finalized at the district level where the district programmes coordinator who may be the district collector or any other district level officer. He consolidates block plans into a district plan and ensures administrative and technical approvals to the shelf of projects. He releases funds and receives utilization certificates. He is also responsible for ensuring hundred per cent monitoring of works, muster roll verifications and submission of monthly progress report. The state Employment Guarantee Council of the state advises the state government on the implementation of the schemes, and evaluates and monitors them. The state government has been made responsible for wide communication of the schemes. It is also the duty of the state government to regularly review, monitor and evaluate NREGS processes and outcomes. The Central Employment Guarantee Council under the chairmanship of the minister of rural development is responsible for advising the central government on NREGS related matters. Moreover, the ministry of rural development is responsible for ensuring timely and adequate resource support to the states and to the Central Council.[25] Besides, adequate numbers of staff from centre to the state and also from the district to the village are involved in giving effect to the NREGS. All payment of NREGA is made through banks or post offices where the workers have to open the account.

Thus, it is obvious that the government with the marked objective to help the unemployed rural unskilled workers launched the NREGA all over the country. This scheme has been appreciated everywhere and it has helped a number of rural workers to improve their living standard. The government is very much generous in allotting funds for implementation of NREGA. Millions of job card holders have been recorded. It has created big hope in the mind of the rural workers. But it is also a reality that the NREGA has to pass through a number of problems that has raised eyebrows all over the country. Firstly, the programme is meant for the unskilled manual workers who are mostly illiterate and ignorant. Many of them do not know how to get the benefit of the programmes and how to obtain job cards. They have to depend upon the government officials related to it or the village brokers who spare nothing to exploit these illiterate workers. Secondly, the economic conditions of the rural workers are so vulnerable that they need work every day, not only 100 days in a year. In search of regular works they have to go far away from the villages. Hence, they remain deprived of the benefits of NREGA. Thirdly, process of payment of wages is also defective. Workers need payment everyday while under the NRGEA they have to wait long for payment. Sometimes payment is made after months due to completion of various processes in this regard. Delay in payment not only puts the workers in trouble but also discourages them to participate in NREGA. A number of cases have come to light where it has been discovered that payment to the workers is not made honestly. Records of works or muster rolls are not maintained properly. In such cases the workers do not know how to correct the errors. Fourthly, with a view to concealing the mishandling of funds, transparency and accountability are not maintained knowingly; last but not the least, cases have come to light that many of the state governments are using the allotted funds for implementation of NREGA. Rather the fund is transferred to other accounts with the result that the workers remain deprived of the benefits of NREGA.

Endnotes

1. *Gramin Vikas News Letter*, Vol. I, No. II, November 1985, Department of Rural Development, op. cit., p.4.
2. *Guidelines of Rural Industries component of IRDP/TRYSEM*, Government of India, Ministry of Rural Reconstruction, December 1979, Annexure I.
3. *TRYSEM, Handbook*, published by Ministry of Rural Development, Government of India, op. cit.
4. Ibid.
5. See Ministry of Rural Reconstruction, Government of India, op. cit. p. 22.
6. Ibid. p. 24
7. Pandey, A.K. (1990), *Local Level Planning and Rural Development*, Delhi, p. 79.
8. *Gramin Vikas Newsletter*, Vol. 5, No. 8-9 August-September, 1989, Department of Rural Development, Ministry of Agriculture, op. cit. p. 22.
9. Ibid.
10. Ibid.
11. Ibid. p. 18.
12. Ibid. p. 18.
13. *Jawahar Rozgar Yojana, Manual*, Department of Rural Development, Ministry of Agriculture, Government of India, New Delhi, 1989, p. 2.
14. Ibid. pp. 216–27.
15. *JRY, Ministry of Agriculture, Rural Development Department*, published by Jamia Milia Islamia, New Delhi, 1989, p. 2.
16. *Gramin Vikas Newsletter*, Vol. 5, No. 8-9, August-September, 1989, Department of Rural Development, Ministry of Agriculture, op. cit. p. 18.
17. *Swarn Jayanti Gram Swarozgar Yojana, Guidelines*, published by the Government of India, Ministry of Rural Development, New Delhi, 1999, p. 1.
18. *Transforming Rural India, Programmes for Change*, published by Ministry of Rural Development, Government of India, New Delhi, 1999, p. 7.

19. Ibid. pp. 7–8.
20. Ibid
21. Ibid.
22. *Transforming Rural India, Programmes for Change*, published by Ministry of Rural Development, Government of India, New Delhi, 1999, pp 18–19.
23. Ibid. p. 22.
24. *The National Rural Employment Guaranteed Act 2005 (NREGA)*, published by the Ministry of Rural Development, Government of India, New Delhi, 2008, p. 2.
25. Ibid. p. 10

Chapter – 6

Bureaucratic Constraints in promoting Socio-Economic Development

Bureaucracy is an indispensable part of a government. The government is known by its administration where different ranks and files of government servants assist the government to prepare new plans and policies and implement them. Bureaucracy reflects the philosophy of the state and government at any particular moment. With the growth of development administration in India not only the administrative infrastructure has been expanded but responsibilities of the bureaucrats have also increased. In a country like India, which is the largest democratic nation whose primary objective is to work for establishment of egalitarian society, the responsibility of the Indian administrators is far greater. India is virtually a country where majority of the people are poor and among the poor the conditions of the poorer are pathetic and vulnerable. India inherited the problems of poverty and unemployment from the British rule. Indian bureaucracy is not a development of post-independence era. India adopted bureaucratic system what it existed during the British rule. During the period of the British rule in India, the entire gamut of development work was carried out not for the sake of the economic development of the nation and its people but to ensure the control of the government over the nation and exploit the natural resources for the benefit of the British people. However, the fact which is notable about the British bureaucracy is that the entire administrative structure was well consolidated, fair, impartial and more or less free from corruption.

After independence the socialist philosophy and centralized planning of the government caused some basic changes in both the organizational structure of bureaucracy and in moral and behavioural character of the bureaucrats. Initiation of development administration in India with a view to improving the rural conditions of the country provided bureaucracy a preferential boost and treatment because it was the real mechanism of government to implement and execute its policies and programmes. Swarn Lata has rightly remarked, "During the period between fifties and eighties, bureaucracy became omnipotent, omnipresent and even omniscient."[1] The inclination of India toward welfare state and attention of the governments to improve the lot of the people specially living in the villages broadened the scope for people's participation in administration on the one hand, and increased the role of bureaucrats to work with the people for their self development on the other. The changing scenario involved the bureaucrats in a large variety of development activities and implementation of thousands of projects throughout the nation. Bureaucracy increased manifolds and almost became bloated. On the other hand, the policy and programmes of development administration increased the power and status of the ruling party (Indian National Congress). Its rulers boasting as fortune makers of the nation, developed undue relations with the bureaucrats and began to interfere in their affairs with the result that the process of politicization of bureaucracy took place. It developed a trend where the bureaucracy began to lose its neutrality and impartiality. To quote Swran Lata once again, "The entire bureaucratic machine during emergency (1975–77) became a pliable tool in the hands of unscrupulous political set-up." Even after lifting of emergency the situation could not improve and "bureaucracy became more and more corrupt."[2]

Application of new regulations, control of increasing infrastructure and their officers, issue of licenses and permits 'assigned unfamiliar duties to the bureaucrats and raised their status among the public. All these created new avenues for them making them stubborn by nature and corrupt by behaviours. This chapter critically analyses the trends, which have recently emerged in Indian administration affecting the development administration.

Changing attitude of Pt. Nehru towards Bureaucrats

Pt. Jawaharlal Nehru, the first prime minister of India, was the man of vision and sympathizers of the poor people. It was he who paved the way for the growth of development administration in India. Pt Nehru even during the phase of freedom struggle was too much vocal about the cause of the poor and assured the people of changing their economic as well social status soon after independence. However, his liberal attitude of reaching out to his countrymen and his soft behaviour towards the bureaucrats did hardly help to change India as per the need. Rather it encouraged corruption among the bureaucrats. He was a bitter critic of ICS officers of India during the British period. He considered them the people of 'narrow and limited outlook', and he wanted that new India must be served by 'earnest efficient workers' who do not give much importance to the 'money motives.' When he became the prime minister, he took the existing administrative structure as "a ship of stare, old, battered, slow moving and unsuited to this age of swift change, which would have to be scrapped and give place to another."[3] However, it is sad to note that he could hardly follow what he thought of before becoming the chief ruler and administrator of the country. However, it does not mean that his commitment towards social change was less. It appears that he himself was fed up with the traditional attitude and style of the Indian bureaucrats. This is evident from his speech, which he delivered in an inaugural address at the 24th annual meeting of the Central Board of Irrigation and Power on 26 October 1953. He looked upon the haphazard proliferation of bureaucracy as a sign of 'mal-development'. He said, "New Delhi is a jungle, a jungle of able men. Still a jungle—you are lost in this jungle of administrative mazes and labyrinths. The way government organizations and departments multiply, lead us nowhere, but to waste."[4]

During the phase of Nehru's rule, the basic emphasis was on industrial development and major chunk of funds was diverted towards that side. No doubt, he borrowed the concept of rural development on the basis of block development from the United States of America by introducing the Community Development Project (CDP), but he never remained firm to one model of administration. Moreover, he never thought of decentralization of power and inclusion of people in rural development. Again, the people who came within the framework of the rural development were mostly farmers. There was no scope at all for the development of the people belonging to the deprived and suppressed sections. Nehru's style of defending bureaucrats was another problem, which not only emboldened the bureaucrats but also made them difficult and proud. Instead of correcting them in time by inflicting exemplary punishment, Nehru called them as 'fine body of men and women' who were 'clean and efficient.' He thought that bureaucrats were highly qualified and civilized people. They had the sense to understand their responsibilities and work for the people. They may not be called 'black sheep', 'mediocre' and 'fools'. It was such approach, which prohibited him from taking stern action against even those civil servants whose guilts were confirmed with the result that the Indian bureaucrats became more and more irresponsible to their responsibilities.

A question may be raised here as to why Pt Nehru did not make efforts to give foundation of a well-disciplined and committed bureaucracy to improve the lot of the country and its people. The answer is that Pt Nehru was a man of farsightedness and his intention to bring about basic change in socio-economic pattern of the country cannot be doubted. He wanted to bring India to the rank of a developed nation. He knew the shortcomings of Indian bureaucrats and their unappreciable style, which they had borrowed from the British regime. Despite all these facts, Nehru did not want to disturb the Indian bureaucrats by taking stern actions against them at the critical juncture through which the country was passing during his time. The partition of India and frequent communal riots between Hindus and Muslims had brought about a number of human problems, which immediately required solutions. Here the bureaucrats had to play greater role. Moreover, the issue of Kashmir had become much more sensitive encouraging other states of India to secede from the Indian federal system. Again, the Chinese aggression in 1962, created numerous problems, which were unexpected. All these situations did not allow Pt Nehru to be tough and rough towards the bureaucrats. Secondly, Pt Nehru was a liberal thinker and democrat by faith. He hardly believed in hard punishment. He preferred the policy of persuasion. Trivedi is quite near to truth about his observation about Nehru's style of administration. He wrote, "His (Nehru's) administrative weaknesses were not so much due to any inertia, indifference or lack of will, as to a psyche, which came to be structured for purposes. He found himself unable to change his way of thinking to suit administrative requirements. His unwillingness to hurt people and his techniques of friendly persuasion and education did not always allow him to stand as a good administrator."[5]

Increasing pace of Corruption among Bureaucrats

Thus, liberal attitude of Pt Nehru towards the bureaucrats left enough scope for corruption in Indian administrative services. Diversion of more funds towards rural development and launching of various development programmes involving the government servants in development works widened the scope for corruption in the country as the years rolled down. Collaboration of bureaucrats with the political leaders further provided push to nepotism.[6] Basudev Panda is of the view, "The corruption prevailing in the ministerial level steadily percolated to the lower levels of administrative work through different stages, contaminating everyone in the hierarchy.[7]

Even during the lifetime of Pt Nehru various cases of corruption came into light where top-ranking ministers both at the Central and state levels were found involved. The ministers played vital role in corrupting the bureaucrats to serve their personal interests. To arrange jobs for their men and issue licences and permits to their wards, they put constant pressure upon the relevant officers who hardly dared to disobey political masters. They hardly heisted to undermine the due process of administrative norms and procedures while serving their interests. Such activities of the ministers encouraged the bureaucrats to take the law in their hands and do what suited them better even at the cost of administration. There is no dearth of examples where the ministers have been found involved in illegal gratification while doing favouratism in getting employment and posting and promotion of the government servants.[8]

Corruption is a vague term. Accepting bribe is not only corruption. In general parlance, corruption means falling down of morality and inclination towards dishonesty to serve personal interests. Corruption, in fact, is a deliberate and international exploitation of one's position, status or resources, directly or indirectly for personal aggrandizement whether it is in terms of material gain or enhancement of power, prestige or influence beyond what is legitimate or sanctioned by commonly accepted norms.[9] According to K Santhanam, the chairman of the Committee on Prevention of Corruption, "any action of failure to take action in the performance of duty by a government servant for some advantage (personal) is corruption." According to Indian Penal Code, whenever a public servant "accepts or obtains or agrees to accept or attempts to obtain from any person for himself or for any other person any gratification" comes under the preview of corruption and he or she "shall be punished with imprisonment of either description for a term which may extend to three years or with fine or with both."[10]

Corruption in Indian administrative system began to raise its head when the Indian political leaders took over power from the British. The administrative system had become considerably weak by the wartime neglect. The situation worsened on account of the departure of a large number of experienced officers of the British root necessitating rapid promotions even of those with little or no merit. Large number of officials was recruited in haphazard manner to fill in the gaps on various scales to handle the expanded activities of the government. In the words of BB Misra, "These were developments, which afforded unscrupulous elements in the public services and politics unprecedented opportunities for acquiring wealth by dubious means."[11] The government tried to check corruption by appointing certain committees and passing the Prevention of Corruption Acts, but it could not be controlled. The sudden extension of the economic activities of the government put into operation a large number of regulations, control mechanism, licenses and permits. These involved a corresponding multiplication of the administrative processes, which broadened the way of administrative actions. For instance, the operational scope of the CDP and NES became so vast that officers at all levels could freely exercise discretion outside the four walls of law. Thus, the union of power and discretion vested at different levels in the execution of development schemes was bound to produce corruption. The stubborn attitude of the government servants and their non-commitment to the works forced the public to pay 'speed money' to the offices concerned to get the work done in time. It was found that even getting order from the higher authorities the officers attached to the lower levels hardly paid any attention until they were "paid appropriate gratification."[12] As stated above, the unwillingness of the government to take appropriate timely action against the corrupt officers increased the amount of corruption.

The reluctance of the higher officials to exercise their discretionary power proved their incompetence. Moreover, a corrupt higher official found he was unable to control his subordinates. Experience and enquiries make it clear that many heads of organizations are themselves corrupt. A corrupt officer can never combat corruption in his organization for fear of his exposure by his subordinates.[13]

Corruption is a common matter in India. No doubt, corruption is common feature of administration all over the world, but in India "its ramifications are so large and pervasive that it has corroded the administrative machinery and retarded efficiency and progress."[14] A general feeling is emerging among the people that development administration in India can never achieve its objectives due to presence of mass corruption. They feel that "with the bureaucratic apparatus with millions of employees, with its legislature, ministers, secretariats, boards and commissions which is a concomitant of a democratic government, it is becoming a heavy burden on the people."[15] This feeling has emerged among the Indian because of massive corruption. To give pace to development administration, the administrative infrastructure from top to bottom has been extended all over the country. The government spends a lot of money on their salaries, allowances etc. There is marked increase in their dearness allowances and other service facilities. However, the government officials are not satisfied. They are ever on the lookout to make extra buck.

Administrative Corruption and Maladministration

In present day administration corruption and maladministration have taken place firm root on large scale. Affirming the truth Santhanam Committee noted that "during the last sixteen years they (ministers) have enriched themselves illegitimately, obtained good jobs for their sons and relations through nepotism." Nepotism and favouritism in the matter of recruitment to public offices is rampant in spite of the instruction of Public Service Commissions. The bright young men and women coming out with high marks from the universities hardly feel confident of getting a post commensurate with their merits and qualifications. It is all because of corruption, which has entered even in the Public Service Commissions at the Centre and the states level. Several cases have come to the light, which clearly show that how the members and the chairmen of the commissions are involved in corruption.

Declining Morality of Government Officials

Another trend, which emerged among the Indian bureaucrats, is decline in their morality. Morality is characteristic of mankind, which is related to inner voice. The whole edifice of a good society is based on high moral character of its people. Morality is the strength of a good man. It binds one to do away with unpleasant things, injurious or harmful to others. An immoral man has no shame. That is why he is always found indulged in immoral acts. So far the morality of bureaucracy is concerned; it is the base of soundness of bureaucracy. The members of bureaucracy are expected to follow strict principles of morality. If moral character of an officer or even minor government officials is weak, it creates doubt and apprehension in the minds of the people as a whole and may malign the image of a good government. It is lust and greed for material prosperity, which makes one morally corrupt. Corruption and morality both are contrary to each other. When morality comes down, corruption is bound to happen.

Continuous decline in moral standard in public life is the serious factor responsible for corrupt practices and in case of India, it has become regular feature. Officials indulge in corruption openly without caring about criticism because they are morally bankrupt. The bureaucrats of good character possess the spirit of self-sacrifice and apply high endeavour to achieve the goal for which they are recruited. The morality of Indian bureaucrats began to decline after the Second World War where they got opportunities to amass wealth by participating in war affairs. In the words of Hoshiar Singh "The material benefits that came from it (war) not only adversely affected the character of those who gained from it enormously in ways legal and illegal, but reduced on the whole the moral calibre of many others. The vast wealth acquired illegally without difficulty and enjoyed freely, without the least apprehension, was a further factor responsible for the decline in the character."[16] Moreover, the declining moral strength of Indian politicians and involvement of ministers in money-making affairs encouraged the Indian bureaucrats to indulge in corruption. They began to misuse power and authority for personal gains.

Nexus between Bureaucratic and Political Corruption

The most harmful and injurious trend which emerged after India's independence is the combination of bureaucratic and political corruption where both bureaucrats and politicians joined hands together to serve their vested interests. This trend has emerged as one of the biggest hurdle in the path of development administration. It has been observed that the bureaucrats "tend to become handmaidens of the politicians" and officials have failed "in their duty to protest or disagree when things are done out of turn and against rules, procedures and public interest."[17] It has also been observed that some bureaucrats occupying the high ranks are so ambitious that they have been found indulging in party and partisan activities. The politicians have established their hold over the lower level officials to serve their purpose. In the words of Nair and Jain "the political and administrative leadership is the fountainhead of corruption."[18] There are senior bureaucrats who for the gain of promotion have fallen in the lap of the ministers. They have been found serving ministers even going down of their status. The Constitution of India has enough provisions for their safeguards. It is not that they served the ministers or politicians out of way due to fear, but to get undue benefits neglecting their bounden duties.

Thousands of crores of rupees sanctioned for implementation of various programmes under development administration have been badly affected by corruption. Goel has rightly remarked that "had these resources been spent properly without leakage at various levels, we would have solved many of our problems in education, healthcare, housing and other areas of social development... We would have been able to make a deeper dent in poverty and unemployment, which have robbed millions of our countrymen of their right to a decent life."[19]

Root of Corruption in Material Prosperity

In the present world there is enough material scope to enjoy life provided one has money. Today, money is considered everything because it is money with which one can buy the means of prosperity and luxuries. Everyone wants to grow rich overnight. Money and material prosperity have not only eaten up morality of man but also has made him mad. The root cause of corruption is the lust for material prosperity; hence, decline in moral standard of the people throughout the society. Corruption has become one of the ills of inefficiency, demoralization and chaos in the country. On 20 November 1996, in the conference of chief secretaries for an effective and responsive administration in India, it was admitted that "the public administration and civil services at all levels were passing through difficult time in terms of eroded credibility and effectiveness of civil service, growing public perception of an unholy nexus between politicians and civil servants and criminals." This clearly indicates that corruption has become the life of the country because of declining moral standard of the people right from upper level to the lower level. Until moral standard of rulers, administrators and people is improved, nothing can help India to achieve the desired goal. Making of laws and amendments in the constitution can never check corruption in the country. BR Ambedakar while taking part the Constituent Assembly debates, stated "The constitution can provide only organizations of the states such as legislature, executive and judiciary. The factors on which the working of these organizations of the state depends are the people and political parties. They will set up as their instruments to carry out their wishes and their politics."[20] But fact is that in India neither the political party is honest to its own ideologies and principles nor their leaders have the ability to guide the nation. Emerging trend of coalition politics in India has nicely illustrated that how politics of defection without any ideological differences has disunited a political party and corrupted its leaders.

Impact of Corruption upon People

Corruption due to decline of moral standard of the bureaucrats and politicians has worried the whole country causing great damage to the policies and programmes of the country, which have been adopted for public welfare and economic development. To quote Goel once again, "There is considerable frustration and dissatisfaction amongst the people, specially the weaker sections of the society, about the apathy, irresponsibility and lack of accountability of the public servants. There is increasing anxiety about growing instances of corruption and criminalization in public life and administration"[21] People belonging to poor, suppressed, deprived and neglected sections of India are losing their faith in the agencies related to development, law and order. In fact their faith "in the registration of offences, their timely investigation and the declining of prompt justice has been eroded."[22]

Corruption in India is a multifaceted problem, which has infected every aspect of life and administration. Starting from the political bosses to the lowest level of bureaucratic functionaries, none seems to be either an exception or immune from its evil effects.[23] Such mounting corruption paving the way for growth of nexus amongst politicians, criminals and bureaucrats have deprived people of benefits of development administration. In 1964, the Committee on Prevention of Corruption in India recorded that the whole country in every sphere and department of life is plunged in the stagnant of ocean of corruption; [24] currently, the amount of corruption has reached the climax. The effect of such corruption is that the people, today, have accepted corruption as a fact of life and becoming accustomed to live with it. Disappointment and depression have entered into their lives. They feel that they can never be liberated from the hard grip of corruption because those who have been assigned with the task to control corruption are themselves corrupt. Until moral value of the bureaucrats, politicians and people is upgraded, the objects with which the development administration has come into being may hardly be achieved.

Notable Factors Involved in Corruption

There are various causes of emergence of corruption in the country. The decline of morality is one of them but the factors like fast growing modernization and industrialization are also responsible for corruption. These two factors have brought about unbridled lust for material prosperity. The civil servants or the government officials find themselves unable to enjoy the modern material facilities with the salaries what they get where prices of the commodities are rising fast. Another factor is lack of public awareness about how to meet the challenges of corruption. The laws, which are available to deal with corruption, are insufficient. Various elements have joined their hands with corruption, among them the notable elements are pressure groups like the Indian Chamber of Commerce, Trade Associations, State Chambers of commerce etc. which are gangs, supposedly the breeders of corruption. They influence "the ruling elites by wining, dining plus providing them other good things of life."[25] Even the judicial system at lower levels, is not functioning efficiently, resulting in delays and corrupt practices. Says Rahul Pathak, "The cost of legislation is exorbitant, the process tedious and the quality of justice given the appalling lack of talents, is suspect."[26] Even the former Chief Justice of the Indian Supreme Court PN Bhagwati, remarked "If the Supreme Court exists only for the rich, what is the use of its existence? I have known judges who have sat on judgment for two years."[27] The number of the cases related to corruption has come into light, which envisages that top ranking bureaucrats along with ministers are involved in various big scandals where millions or crores of rupees have been pocketed. The investigation, which is going against them, is not encouraging. These corrupt elements have developed proximity with the corrupt authorities to manage their safe release and obtain a clean chit.

Another factor which emerged in the Indian administrative sector is impact and influence of the Indian industrial and commercial classes and the interests of the ministers, legislators and party officials. Santhanam committee found that possession of "large amount of unaccounted money by various persons including those belonging to the industrial and commercial classes is a major impediment in the purification of public life." He further observed "If anti-corruption activities are to be successful, it may be recognized that it is as important to fight these unscrupulous agencies of corruption as to eliminate corruption in the public service, but, in fact, they go togotehr."[28] The vested elements belonging to industrial and commercial houses spared nothing to mobilize the rulers and bureaucrats to serve their interests by offering good amount of money and material benefits. Acceptance of presentations in the form of material and money offered to the high officials or their temptation towards the life of luxuries and comforts degraded them from the path of morality. They became stooge of the vested interests. This encourages the officers and the officials of lower classes who keeping aside their morality indulge themselves in practice of corruption openly.

In fact, various trends including corruption emerged in Indian administrative system on large scale with the introduction of new economic policies in India. The second Five-Year Plan, which proceeded on the lines indicated in the industrial policy resolution of 1956, saw corruption growing into an organized force. By 1960, the number of cases investigated by the Delhi police establishment alone increased almost two-fold in about ten years[29] pointing to the growing amount of corruption among the bureaucrats, which attracted the attention of media, parliament and public. By the time the Santhanam Committee was appointed in September 1962, corruption had increased to an extent where people had started losing faith in the integrity of public administration itself, not excluding even its decision-making political apparatus.[30]

The Santhanam Committee noted that the existing rules governing the conducts of public servants were more or less unchanged from those existing prior to the commencement of the Constitution. The Committee as a remedial measure suggested assigning specific responsibility upon the superior officers to keep a watchful eye on the integrity of their subordinates. Every government servant must take full responsibility for his own action and orders except when acting under the direction of his superiors. This provided an opportunity to the subordinate officers to protect them from bearing responsibility under the plea that what they did was under the direction of their superiors.

Several cases have come in the light where big government officials have been found doing favours to the big business managements or enterprises because of personal gains from those firms. Confirming the same fact, Nair and Jain say that "there have also been many cases in which it has been found that while in office, they (government officials) have helped a particular business or industrial house in many ways."[31] The report of the Sarkar Committee contained serious charges against high officials of the Iron and Steel ministry. Cases have also been found where the officials after their retirement got employment in the firms which they had benefited during their tenure of the government service. The Santhanam Committee recorded that a large number of high officials are incorruptible but the businessmen "make a careful study of the character, tastes and weaknesses of officials with who they may have to deal and these weaknesses are then exploited. The tendency to subvert integrity in the public service instead of being isolated and abortive is growing into an organized, well-planned racket."[32]

The government of India set up the Central Bureau of Investigation (CBI) in 1963 in the ministry of home affairs with the purpose to deal with the case of bribery, corruption, misconduct of central government personnel, breaches of law etc. During the year 1990–91 the CBI registered 1180 cases, out of which 964 cases were against the public servants and the remaining against the private persons/firms. In 1991, it handled 2409 cases where 933 officers were involved in 633 cases. The CBI found itself unable to deal with all these cases properly and take timely action. The government also set up Central Vigilance Commission to meet the purpose, but that, too, did not bring down the rate of corruption in the country. Despite several steps taken by the government to curb down corruption and correct the administrative machinery, the attitude and behaviour of the government servants awaits to be corrected.

Public Awareness in Changing Atmosphere

According to Divya Thakur "Our bureaucrats seem averse to adopt themselves to changing times. They tend to be dogmatic rather than being flexible and amenable to new ideas and innovations."[33] Today scenario has totally changed. With the spread of mass democracy and emerging consciousness of people and their participation in development administration after decentralization of power and introduction of Panchayati Raj, public administration demands total change in the attitude and behaviour of the public servants. Right to information, judicial activism, increasing pluralism in civil society with the strengthening of professions and appearance of non-governmental organizations are posing challenges to the bureaucracy with the changing environments. Bureaucracy needs to be resilient enough to observe and react to those changes. Need of time where much more emphasis has been laid down on development administration and welfare state is timely and prompt action. The implementation of programmes needs speed and efficiency. What is urgently needed is to train the bureaucrats keeping in view the changing circumstance. According to Pandey "They (bureaucrats) must be made to realize that they have to serve the people and not their aggrandizement They must be at the doorstep of the people all the time and if they fail, they must bear the brunt."[34]

In his address delivered on IIPA'S, on 29 March 1999 the then Prime Minister Atal Behari Vajpayee, expressed the view that his close observation of working of administrative system in India was not satisfactory. Said he, "My observation both from outside and inside have left me in no doubt that our system of administration is ill-equipped to fulfill our rational objectives and the aspirations of the common man." What the then prime minister remarked indicates that the system of administration in India is sick, needing immediate cure. It must be responsive, transparent, efficient and caring. It should respond to people's concerns. Its functions should be open and accountable. Honesty and ability to decide between the right and the wrong are qualities as important as professional competence. Ravishankar and Jayanthi expressed, "It should be compassionate. In a country where vast majority of the people are victims of poverty and neglect, we have to have an administrative system that has a heart that feels for the poor and a mind that cares for their needs."[35]

Development administration today, demands application of technologies to industries, agriculture, transportation etc. Again, it demands people's participation on large scale from the grassroots levels in decision making and in the fields of allocation of resources (planning) in the determination of conditions of work (management) and in improving standards of living (distribution). Bureaucry, today, has become a director and a regulator of activities in society because more or less each aspect of life of citizens in a society is subject of state regulation and assistance. Bureaucracy has emerged as an instrument of state action spreading its tentacles. Hence, it must be more responsive and accountable.

It was Mrs. Indira Gandhi who while launching the development programmes and schemes on large scale, introduced the idea of committed bureaucracy, but not to the people, but to the individual politician in power rather than to the principles of the constitution and the letter of the law. Since the seventies the politicization of the administration has preceded apace.[36] According to PS Appu offices of the IAS and the IPS have shown "a marked tendency to carry out the wishes of their political masters without pausing to consider if the contemplated action is in accordance with the law. Many of them have behaved like the servile, not as the members of the law of the land maintaining the principles of democratic governance."[37]

Thus, the close proximity between the politicians and the bureaucrats to serve their personal interest has badly affected the progress and success of development administration all over the country. Since the civil servants have political patronage, they hardly care for any complaint or allegation. Such trends, which have emerged in Indian administrative system right from top to bottom, have made the government servants more irresponsible and arrogant. They hardly care to take timely action. They knowingly delay the decision. Files hardly move in time. The officers and employees belonging to any class, categories or position, sit over the files as long as they wish according to their whims and fancies. Since there is no effective provision for time limit to deal the file, they take undue benefits of such administrative loopholes. Any officer or employees due to selfish interests or being incompetent can conveniently raise any inconsequential query and delay the case for its disposal. Such officers may either be punished or transferred, but they have the scope to manage cancellation of their transfers by offering money to their controlling officers or even by approaching their political mentors. What the country needs today, is a complete "overhauling of bureaucracy in terms of its attitudinal and structural patterns for it to play a constructive role in the 21st century."[38]

Rise of Corruption despite various Correcting Methods

The administrative pattern of India is based on sound principles and the government adopted various measures to check corruption but no; the corruption among the government officials has spread like an epidemic. There is no department of the government or office which is immune to the disease of corruption. The question is why has the corruption increased despite various stringent measure in force?

The most valid answer is lack of administrative ethics among the government officials and lack of hard determination of the government to weed out corruption. Ethics according to the *Concise Oxford Dictionary* is "the science of morals in human conduct; moral philosophy; moral principles and rule of conducts". When ethics of an administrator declines, his faith in moral principles or good conducts begins to disappear. Moral values are indispensable for good governance. Efficient and technologically sound administrative machinery, unless it stands on high moral pedestal, does not serve the public; rather it serves a self-perpetuating and exploitative system. The comments and remarks regarding the administrative performances of the country given by the Indian judiciary and mass media explicitly prove that the Indian administrators and government servants are suffering from low morality. Public men, whatever their status should lead from the public;besides, politicking must stop. Lack of morality has corrupted each aspect of public life. Under such corrupt environment there cannot be any development until the government machinery is moralized. However, the reality is that instead of rise in morals of the government servants they are becoming immoral day by day.

Moreover, criminal elements who have entered into politics and administration, are posing serious danger to rule of law; according to Goel, the people are coerced to follow the dictates of criminals, thus giving rise to violence, unrest and explosive situations."[39]

Ethics is the prime mover of a welfare state. Today, the problems, which have emerged before the people of India are due to lack of administrative ethics. Moral values are values that tell us what is the right, proper and acceptable way of behaviour. India cannot boast of high moral standards because morality of the country has gone deep down not only in administrative hierarchy but even in political arena. Panda is very much correct in his observation that no drive against corruption can succeed until the government itself is firmly committed to the task of weeding out dishonest and corrupt officials, irrespective of rank and status. Punishment for corruption should be exemplary, the least being dismissal from service.[40] The government should also assure that anti-corruption agencies are manned by personnel of unquestionable integrity. [41]

During the colonial period though the bureaucracy was not representative, its ethics were very high. There were good manners and relations between the government and the civil servants, but not for personal gains, but for efficiency in rule and order. Neither the ruler compelled the bureaucrats to deviate from the ethical standard for personal political gain nor did the bureaucrats expect undue favours from the rulers.[42]

In fact there was no subservience, no lack of frankness in advice. There was no reason for any civil servant to feel any sense of inferiority before his political chief. After independence, with the expanding scope of public administration under the marked objective of welfare state and socialistic pattern of society, the number of bureaucrats increased, but their moral standard decreased. Inclusion of inadequately qualified officers in the civil service and reservation of seats for minorities and their recruitment with low quality paved the way for the growth of declination of administrative ethics. On the other hand, the quality of ministers went on declining day by day. According to BB Misra, ministers happened to be men not merely without administrative experience, but also without the romantic halo of political sufferings. The only basis of obedience to the orders of such minister was their legal authority to decide, an authority not based on morality or character."[43] The decline in the standard of ministerial efficiency either encouraged functional pervasion through bureaucratic overtones in policy direction, or led to an abuse of bureaucratic initiative in sub-serving the interest of an individual or a group. What suffered in either case was the democratic principle of ministerial responsibility to the legislature.

Ministers and Bureaucrats

A pertinent question rises as to who should be blamed for downward trend in the administrative performances in India. Are ministers responsible or bureaucrats for declining moral standard in administrative system? Ministers and bureaucrats both are equally responsible for deteriorating administrative ethics, but there are several other factors too, which have affected soundness of administration. Ministers who come from different constituencies on the basis of caste and religion politics wish to appease the electorate even at the cost of administrative sanctity. They hardly hesitate to bypass the norms of administration for which they unnecessarily put pressure upon their respective secretaries to mishandle the administrative machinery for serving ministerial interests.

Secondly, the secretaries who are close to the ministers dare not oppose the political bosses because their future promotion and other interests would be fulfilled only if they are in the good books of their minister.. It has been observed, in many cases, that the secretaries generally accept even the wrong viewpoints of ministers either because of their unwillingness to displease the minister by giving right advice or to appease him by accepting wrong direction to get his patronage and favour. Thirdly, it has also been seen that the individual or the group concerned with the matter directly approach the minister bypassing the bureaucratic head. In this regard BB Misra has rightly remarked, "A tendency naturally grows to look not to one's immediate superior for redress of grievances or for promotion, but to approach the minister direct over the heads of bureaucrats. This has brought about a situation where administrative authority stands eroded beyond repair."[44]

Today, the most dangerous factor, which has created a big rift between the political executive and the bureaucrats, is politicization of administration. The threshold of bureaucracy, which was very much strong and tight during the British rule has been opened to all with the result that the elements that have entered in the bureaucratic framework have created numerous problems by undermining the significance of administrative system. The reservation of seats or quota for schedule castes and scheduled tribes and backward classes has enabled the members of such categories to have their share in the administration but at the cost of standard of bureaucracy. Reservations in jobs and academic institutions are not a boon but a bane. Presently, the recruits of reservation and quota occupy the high hierarchal rank of bureaucracy; these recruits are spineless and lack guts to call a spade a spade and hardly dare to oppose the ministers to the face of a minister boss and submit to his high-handedness and undue interference in administrative system. As a result, the ministers for their personal interests are mounting over the bureaucrats. The bureaucratic capacity to resist for right cause has come down due to erosion of its authority and reduction of capability. Not only that, even corruption has taken place in the system of recruitment and appointment of the civil servants with the result that new entrants in the civil services are found lacking in required calibre and capacity to deal with the problems effectively.

The development of relationship of mutual respect between politicians and officials is necessary for both economic progress and democratic development. During the colonial period the relationship between the politicians and officials was not smooth. Moreover, the district officials paid much attention to ensure law and order, the provision of justice, the collection of taxes, development functions and the hearing of the grievances and the settlement of the disputes in the community. Currently, the district staff has many more functions to perform as a result of significant increase in the development activities. After independence the situation has changed. At present, there is no direct conflict between these two forces, but the politicians or members to the ruling party(s) are dominating over the officials to such an extent that the officials are afraid to do anything that may displease prominent local party men because they have close link with the ministers. Several cases have come to the light where the local politicians have been found to pressurize the district officials to do as directed. In case of officials' refusal, they do not hesitate to serve warnings to such officers. In order to have both good administration and good government, Khera suggests, "There should be considerable interpenetration between the political party and those representing authority on the hand and administrative function and power on the other,"and that the bureaucracy "should avoid any rigid attitude about the exclusiveness of the administrative services and the administrative staffs from the play of political events."[45]

It has been observed that due to politicization of administration and collaboration of the administrator with the ruling politicians the opposition members criticize it and generally blame the administrators. This has created a peculiar situation for the government officials. According to Nair and Jain, the district officers are often rewarded only with abuse and the enmity of all parties and factions. The administration is a scapegoat in political conflicts (between the ruling and opposition parties);[46] the increased bitterness of factional strife in the district political organization and the existence of sharply defined groups in the district have "made administrators wary of identifying themselves with particular factions." To quote Nair and Jain, "When state ministers are directly involved, then the district staff has no choice but to obey the directives of their ministers." The study reflects the truth that what has been in the recent years is that the ministers in the state government have used their officers in the district for their own political purposes.[47]

High-handedness of Central Agencies

The trend which has appeared among the members of the Indian Planning Commission is also serious. The members are not experts, but ideologues of socialism. It is not an advisory body outside government but a branch of the government and has all the prestige and power given by the prime minister, the planning minister and the finance minister. It has become a regular department of the government and the members of the Planning commission enjoy all the privileges of a minister. Besides the Planning Commission, there are National Development Council, and other Central agencies of the same nature. All these agencies are supported with vast army of clerks and other related officials. All these provisions have not only created the problem of overlapping of the plans but also delay in formulation of plans.

There is lack of coordination among various departments of the government that are related to the developmental works. This causes delay in policy formulation and its implementation. Even after a decision has been taken, there are no levels found specifically responsible for ensuring the effective implementation of the decision. Instead, the matter ends with the communication of decision to the field administration. About supervision, it has been "found that all supervision is carried out in a ritualistic manner and that too at lower levels." Lack of strict disciplinary action against the corrupt officials has encouraged them to indulge in corrupt affairs fearlessly.

The lacunae the administrations in India suffer from are "too much examination and scrutiny before a decision is actually arrived at. But surprisingly enough, there are few rules and procedures to review, to scrutinize and to evaluate the actions taken after a decision have been arrived at."[48] During implementation of the plans or schemes, occasions appear which need immediate solution for that immediate decision is required. The officers concerned are in confusion about taking decision due to lack of clear cut provision or power of delegation in this regard. As a result the public works hamper.

Thus, it is obvious that various trends, which have emerged in the administrative system of India, have directly or indirectly maligned the significance of administration on the one hand, and harmed the progressive programmes and policies of the government on the other. No doubt, there are still some administrators who possess the worth and quality, but their number is limited and they are found helpless to help the public. Such honest and initiator officers, be they IAS or IPS are punished rather than rewarded. When the vested interests complain against such honest officers, they see to it that they are either transferred or shunted to the places, where their qualities and abilities rot.

The subordinate officers deployed to various ranks and files in the districts, blocks and sub-divisions are mostly corrupt. They are in direct contact with the public. They have created ample avenues to take bribes from the public even for petty things. The officers above them are also corrupt. Instead of having effective control over subordinate officers, they demand their share form subordinate officers who are directly involved in moneymaking business. As a result, bribery, commission and gifts etc. have taken the white shape today. The people who are illiterate, and who have no approach to higher authority or minister, are deprived of the due benefits of development administration. They do not know what to do and where to go for redressal of their grievances. In such situations they have to totally depend upon the brokers who in the name of help usurp their major benefits by cheating and deceiving them. Such brokers establish some sort of relations with the concerned officials and manage to get the work done on the condition that the benefits of welfare programmes would be shared. Thus, rural poor are deprived of the major chunk of benefits of rural development programmes such as Indira Awas Yojana, Old Age Pension, Schemes of loans on various accounts with subsidies etc.

Due to mass corruption prevailing in the country from top to buttom the aims and objectives of the development administration have not been achieved. There is no denying the fact that the government has launched many schemes and projects to eradicate poverty from India and millions of rupees have been spent over such programmes. But it cannot be denied that poverty in India has not been eradicated. Rather the gap between the rich and the poor has increased. A section of the people who are either in the government or having close contact with the government servants have amassed enormous quantity of wealth and leading the life of luxury and comforts. On the other side, there are millions of people who barely eke out a living for their children. Millions are yet homeless and many of them have no means to earn their livelihood. It appears that they were born to suffer and perish.

Bureaucrats tend to become handmaidens of the politicians and officials have failed in their duty to raise the voice of protest or disagreement when things are done out of turn and against rules, procedures and public interests. The corrupt high officials find themselves unable to put effective control over their subordinates. Continuous decline in moral standard in public life, which has become the regular feature of India, is the serious factor responsible for corrupt practices. Like the politicians, moral standard of government officials has also gone down. Various scams we witness currrently prove that the ministers and bureaucrats have bid goodbye to morality to engage in moneymaking pursuits at the cost of the nation and its people. Cases have also come to light, which prove that big government officials are doing favours to the big business houses because of personal gains from those firms. The government officials belonging to any grade or cadre delay movement of file as long as they are not bribed as per their wish. Such officials are rarely punished due to their close proximity with the higher officials or ministers. Another trend which has harmed the development administration is politicization of administration, wherein the administrators are the middlemen of the ministers.

The socially, economically and educationally backward poor people of rural India have not yet fully understood the meaning and significance of the development programmes. The programmes provided them with some jobs but only for limited days. Unless they are given employment for the whole year, they cannot come out of the grip of poverty. Due to growing selfish elements such as brokers who are always on the lookout to take the undue benefits of the illiterate rural labourers, have cheated them. Moreover, the government officials related to such programmes have not come ahead to help the unfortunate lot. Rather, the discretionary powers exercised by different categories of government officials opened up scope for harassment, malpractices and corruption. It is true that development administration during recent years has provided some sort of economic relief to the poor and unemployed, but that is a temporary relief. It cannot solve their problems for ever.

A close observation and analysis of working of development administration brings to fore that the government while introducing the PRI decentralized the power, but this did not change the mindset of bureaucrats. Sharma and Misra rightly say, "With a view to forestalling the dangers of bureaucratism elitism and the totalitarianism, people's participation becomes imperative".[49] A survey of the study reveals the facts that the bureaucrats and government officials attached to the rural development administration hardly remained committed to the spirit so essential for success of the programmes. Various studies in this field made by different agencies and institutions also concluded that the majority of benefits of rural development programmes have been unduly taken by the vested interest due to their collaboration with the officers concerned. Study also reveals that the PRIs have always been under the dominance of economically and socially privileged sections of the society.

The most dangerous trend which has appeared is mass corruption among the government officials who under the patronage of political leaders hardly hesitate to indulge in corrupt practices in the field of rural development. Expanding infrastructure and growth in the scope of administration due to advent of development administration have brought about various set of new rules and regulations thereby increasing the discretionary powers of the bureaucrats and government servants. The power of decentralization has provided them with enough scope to handle the affairs as they like. All these have made them irresponsible and obstinate with the result that the villagers do not get required cooperation from such officers. The subordinate officers delay the action knowingly and wait for bribes. All anti-corruption measures have failed to control such officers because they are morally corrupt including Mukhyas, Pradhans, BDOs, COs, Gram Sevaks, VLDs. The trends which have emerged in the system of Indian administration have hampered the affairs. These have directly or indirectly maligned the significance of administration on the one hand, and affected the progressive policies of the government on the other. There are some honest and committed officers, but their number is limited. Moreover, political interference in their affairs hardly allows them to follow the course of fit and proper action. Instead of getting appreciation for their good works, they are served with punishments like transfer, suspension, scolding etc. which dampen their spirit and courage.

The government of India from the inception of the democratic rule in the country has been talking more than enough to work for the poor and remove poverty from the country but the results which one sees in this regard are different. Neither poverty has been removed nor have the poor been helped out according to their needs. Every government since independence has spouted the slogan of *'Garibi Hatao'* in some manner, shape or form. But according to Malvik Singh, "neither the left, nor the right, nor centre did anything for the 'poor' or for that matter for anyone other than their own reserve tribe, once they sat on the treasury benches." He further remarks that monies allocated in plan upon plan never reached the people at the 'grassroots'. Only a trickle happened. The bulk of all allocations were chewed up by rulers and their administrators, regardless of 'colour'emblem or flag."[50] There may be some exaggeration in the statement of Singh but his observation about the results of poverty alleviation programmes are very much near to the truth.

Despite all this, the Government of India as well as the state governments must be appreciated for their concern and efforts to think about poverty alleviation schemes and programmes and allotment of funds for development of the poor and needy persons. Such efforts and policies of the government have sharpened the awareness of the rural people and made them active to work for their self-development. Their attitude towards poverty has changed now. They have realized that until they work hard and avail the opportunities provided by the government for self-development, their troubles and problems will never come to an end. Lacs of rural poor who were homeless have got their own home under the provision of the Indira Awas Yojana. Millions of people have been involved in works under the programmes launched under the JRY, SGSY, JGSY etc. If corruption is checked and mindset of the government officials undergoes a change, there is no doubt that the policies and programmes of the government may play a vital role in removing poverty from the country and helping all those who are still deprived of the national benefits. There is also an immediate need to make the rural people more aware of the government policies and programmes, which have come in practice for their development.

Endnotes

1. Swarn Lata, *Indian Bureaucracy since Liberalization*, in Bhartwal C P., & Kishore K., (eds),(2003) *Public Administration in India: Current Perspectives*, APH Publishers Corporation, New Delhi, p. 92.
2. Ibid. p. 93
3. Singh Tarlok, (1969), *Towards an Integrated Society: Reflection on Planning social Society and Rural Institutions,* Orient Longman, New Delhi, p. 363.
4. Narasimha, C.D., (ed) (1960), *India's spokesman, from Speeches and Addresses of Pt. J. Nehru,* Macmillan, pp. 85–90.
5. Trivedi, K D., (1987), *Perspective in Development Administration,* Mittal Publications, New Delhi, p. 30.
6. *Report on the Committee of Prevention of Corruption*, Para-2, 16, Ministry of Home Affairs, Government of India, New Delhi, 1964.

7. Basudev Panda, (1978), *Indian Bureaucracy*, New Delhi, p. 96.

8. Verma S.P., "Corruption and Political Development in India", *Political Science Review*, Vol. 13, No 1-4, January-December, 1974, p. 172.

9. Avasthi and Maheshwari (1971), *Public Administration in India*, Agra, p. 342.

10. Indian Penal Code, Section 161.

11. Misra, B.B., *Government and Bureaucracy in India*, op. cit. p. 274.

12. *Report of the Santhanam committee of India*, published by the Government of India, March 1964, p. 10.

13. *Report of the Rural-Urban Relationship*, published by the Government of India, 1966, pp. 11-10.

14. Nair Jeevan and Jain U.C., (2000),) *The Indian Bureaucratic System*, Pointer Publishers, Jaipur, p. 176.

15. Ibid.

16. Singh Hoshiar (Ed) (11985), *Rural Development in India*, Jaipur, p. 109.

17. Nair Jeevan and Jain UC., (2000), *The Indian Bureaucratic system*, Pointer Publishers, Jaipur. p. 176.

18. Ibid. p. 177.

19. Goel S.L., (2003), *Advanced Public Administration*, Deep and Deep Publications, New Delhi, p. 536.

20. Constituent Assembly Debates, Vol. XI, No. 1, November, 1949, p. 975.

21. Goel S.L., (2003), *Advanced Public Administration*, op. cit. p.537.

22. Ibid.

23. Sharma, S.K., (1991), *Corruption in Indian Politics and Bureaucracy*, New Delhi, p. 123.

24. Report on the Committee of Prevention of Corruption, Para-2, 16, Ministry of Home Affairs, Government of India, New Delhi, 1964. p. 216.

25. Goel S.L., (2003), *Advanced Public Administration*, op. cit. p.545.

26. Pathak Rahul, "The Judiciary Grumbling Citadel", in *India Today,* June 30, 1992.

27. Ibid.

28. *Report of the Santhanam Committee of India*, published by the Government of India, March 1964, pp. 10-11.

29. Ibid. 12.

30. Ibid. p. 7

31. Nair Jeevan and Jain U C., (2000), *The Indian Bureaucratic system,* Pointer Publishers, Jaipur. P. 177.

32. Ibid. p. 178.

33. Thakur Divya, "Bureaucracy and Liberalization in India", in Nair Jeevan and Jain U.C., *The Indian Bureaucratic system* (2000), Pointer Publishers, Jaipur. p. 176.p. 147

34. Pandey J., "Bureaucracy in Bihar: A Surgical Operation on Gandhian Line", and Jain UC., (2000), Pointer Publishers, Jaipur. p. 175.

35. Quoted in Bhartwal C P and Kishore K, (ed) *Public Administration in India: Current Perspective,* op. cit., p. 168.

36. Guha R., "Politics and Play", *The Telegraph*, April, 2, 2005, p. 8.

37. Cited in Ibid, p. 8.

38. Usha K., "Challenge of Bureaucracy in India since Independence", in *Public Administration in India* edited by Bhartwal and Kishore K, op. cit., p. 143.

39. Goel S.L., (2003), *Advanced Public Administration,* op. cit. p.753.

40. Panda Basudev, *Indian Bureaucracy*, op. cit., pp. 146–47.

41. Rai Hand Singh S P., (1979), *Current Ideals and Issues in Indian Administration,* New Delhi, p. 209.

42. Gorwala, (1952), *The Role of Administrators: Present, Past and Future*, Poona, p. 12.

43. Misra B B., *Government and Bureaucracy in India,* op. cit., p. p. 117.

44. Ibid. p. 174.
45. Nair Jeevan and Jain U C., (2000), *The Indian Bureaucratic system,* Pointer Publishers, Jaipur. p. 231.
46. Ibid. p.232.
47. Ibid. p. 233.
48. Nair Jeevan and Jain U C., (2000), *The Indian Bureaucratic system,* Pointer Publishers, Jaipur. pp. 231-33.
49. Sharma S.N & Misra K., "Insuring People's Participation in Rural Development", op. cit., p.6
50. Singh Malvik, "Time to Call the Bluff", in the *Telegraph* (Guwahati), August 23, 2005.

Bibliography

PRIMARY SOURCES

1. Some importnat Government files related to Bureaucracy and Development Administration.
2. Proceedings of the Government of India in Home, Establishment, Judicial and Political Department.
3. Proceedings of Indian National Congress 1929, 1931, 1932, 1940 and 1942.
4. Bengal Judicial Proceedings.
5. Secretariat of Governor-General file No.-119/45 (Reorganization of Services to Post-war Conditions, Para-2.
6. Home (Medical) File No. 41 of March 1885.
7. Home (Estt.), A Progs, Nos. 141/34 Confidential, Simla Report, 3.
8. Rules of Procedure and Conduct of Business in Lok Sabha, Lok Sabha Secretariat, New Delhi, 1957. New Delhi.
9. Jawahar Rozgar Yojna (JRY), a Manual issued by the Department of Rural Development, Ministry of Agriculture, GOIU. New Delhi, 1989.

10. Swarnjayanti Gramin Swarozgar Yojna, a booklet published by the Ministry of Rural Development GOI, New Delhi, 1999.

11. TRYSEM, a Handbook, published by the Ministry of Rural Development, GOI, New Delhi, 1980.

12. Gramin Vikas Newsletter, a weekly magazine, published by the Ministry of Rural Development, GOI, New Delhi, 1980.

GOVERNMENT'S PUBLICATIONS

1. Constituent Assembly Debates, 1946, 1947, and 1948, Government of India Publication, New Delhi.

2. Proceedings of the Lok Sabha published by the Library of Indian Parliament.

3. 1st Five Year Plan. Planning Commission of India, New Delhi.

4. 2nd Five Year Plan. Planning Commission of India. New Delhi.

5. 2nd Five Year Plan. Planning Commission of India. New Delhi.

6. 4th Five Year Plan. Planning Commission of India. New Delhi.

7. 5th Five Year Plan. Planning Commission of India. New Delhi.

8. 6th Five Year Plan. Planning Commission of India. New Delhi.

9. 7th Five Year Plan. Planning Commission of India. New Delhi.

10. 8th Five Year Plan. Planning Commission of India. New Delhi.

11. 9th Five Year Plan. Planning Commission of India. New Delhi.

12. 10th Five Year Plan. Planning Commission of India. New Delhi.

13. Constitution of India. Allahabad Law Agency. Allahabad. 1965.

14. The All India Service Act. 1951. No. LXI of 1951.

15. The Government of India Act, 1935.

16. Shiva Rao. B. (Ed.). *The Framina of India's Constitution.* Vol. I to IV. Indian Institute of Public Administration. New Delhi. 1968.

17. *Community Development, Panchayati Raj and Cooperative. Publication Division.* Government of India. New Delhi. 1964.

18. Annual Report of the Ministry of Home Affairs. Department of Administrative Reforms. Government of India. New Delhi.

19. Report of the ARC Study Team on Machinery of Government of India and Procedure of Work. Vol. I. II. III. IV. published by the Department of Rural Development. GOI. New Delhi.

SECONDARY SOURCES

BOOKS

1. Agrawal S N. 1946. *Gandhian Constitution of Free India.* Allahabad.

2. Agrawal R C. 1965. *National Movement and Constitutional Development of India.* Metropolitan Book Company. New Delhi.

3. Ali Sadia. 1979. *Indian National Congress. Resolution on Economic Policy.* Programme and Allied Matters. 1924-1969. Oxford Publications. New Delhi.

4. Arora Ramesh K (Ed.) 1979. *Perspective in Administrative Theory.* I.I.P.A. New Delhi.

5. Asok Chand. 1958. *Indian Administration.* Penguin. London.

6. Austin. G. 1972. *The Indian Constitution.* Metro Publications. Delhi.

7. Avasthi A. 1980. *Central Administration.* Vishal Publications. New Delhi.

8. ------------ 1972. *The Municipal Administration in India.* Lakshmi Narayan Agrawal Publications. Agra.

9. Avasthi A & Maheshwari S.R. 1986. *Public Administration.* Lakshmi Narayan Agrawal Publications. Agra.

10. Blan Peter M. 1962. *Bureaucracy in Modern Society.* Random House. New York.

11. Banerjee. M. 1968. *Planning in India.* Deep and Deep Publications. New Delhi.

12. Bata K. Dev. 1978. *Bureaucracy, Development and Public Management in India.* Uppal Publications. New Delhi.

13. Basu Durga Das. 1978. *An Introduction to the Constitution of India.* Vivek Publications. New Delhi.

14. ------------- 1877. *Constitutional Law of India.* Vivek Publications. New Delhi.

15. Bhargava. G.S. 1971. *A Study of Political Corruption in India.* Delhi.

16. Bhambri. C.P. 1972. *Administrators in Changing Society.* National Publishing House. New Delhi.

17. Bhaskara Rao. V. 1990. *Public Administration in India.* Ajanta Publications. New Delhi.

18. Bhattacharya. M. 1971. *Public Administration: Structure, Process and Behaviour.* Kolkata.

19. Bhale Rao. C.N. (Ed.) 1972. *Administration, Politics and Development in India.* Bombay.

20. Bhartwal C.P and Kumar Kishore 2003, *Public Administration in India, Current Perspective.* A.P.H. Publishing Corporation. New Delhi.

21. Blunt Sir Edward. 1939. *Social Service in India.* Princeton, London.

22. Braibani Ralph (Ed.). 1963. *Administration and Economic Development.* Oxford. London.

23. Burke. B. John. 1986. *Bureaucratic Responsibility.* Baltimore John Hopkins University Press. London.

24. Chaudhary Roy. 1992. *Sociology of Public Administration.* Calcutta.

25. Cole. G.D.H. *Socialism in Evolution.* Oxford. London.

26. Copland. R. 1943. The Indian Problem-1839-1935. *Report on the Constitutional Problem in India.* Part-I. London.

27. Das. R.D. (Ed.) 1968. *Deliberative and Executive Wins in Local Government.* Calcutta.

28. Darda. R.S. 1985. *Local Government : A Comparative Study.* Jodhpur.

29. Dandekar. V.M. & Nilkanth Rath. 1971. *Poverty in India.* Bombay.

30. Datta Prabhat Kumar. 1981. *Public Administration and the State.* Uppal Publications. New Delhi.

31. Dwarka Das. R. 1960. *Role of Higher Civil Servants in India.* Bombay.

32. Dwivedi. O.P. and R.B. Jain. 1986. *Administration in State.* Gitanjali Publishing Houe. New Delhi.

33. *Encyclopedia of Social Science.* Vol. I. Editor Jonathan Michie. 2001. Fitzrov Dearborn. London.

34. Gauldner. Alwin W. 1955. *Pattern of Industrial Bureaucracy.* Rutledge and Kegon Paul London.

35. Gerth. H. N. & Wright Mills C. (Ed.). 1946. *Bureaucracy from Max Weber : Essay in Sociology.* Oxford University Press. New York.

36. Gorwala, A.D. 1952. *Report on Public Administration.* New Delhi.

37. Gorwala. A.D. 1952. *The Role of the Administra or, Past, Present and Future.* Poona.

38. ------------ 1954. *Report on the Efficient Conducts of State Enterprises.* Delhi.

39. Gowda. K.S. 1972. *Urban and Regional Planning.* Mysore.

40. Goel. S.L. 2003. *Advanced Public Administration,* Deep and Deep Publications. New Delhi.

41. Hanson. A.H. 1966. *The Process of Planning.* London.

42. ------------ 1969. *The Crisis of Indian Planning.* London.

43. Heady Ferrell. 1989. *Public Administration: A comparative Perspective.* Prentice Hall. London.

44. ICSSR. 1973. *A Survey of Research in Public Administration.* Allied Publication. New Delhi.

45. *International Encyclopedia of Social Science. Vol. I.* 1972. Macmillan. London.

46. Inamdar. N.R. 1992. *Development Administration in India.* Rawat Publication. New Delhi.

47. Jain R.B. 1976. *Contemporary Issues in Indian Public Administration.* Vishal Publications. New Delhi.

48. ------------ 2001. *Administration in India: Challenges for Good Governance.* Deep and Deep Publications. New Delhi.

49. Jain. H. M. 1969. *The Union Executive.* Allahabad.

50. Jain. S.C. 1967. *Community Development and Panchayati Raj in India.* Delhi.

51. Jennings. S.I. 1959. *Cabinet Government in England.* Cambridge University Press. London.

52. ------------ 1963. *Some Characteristics of the Indian Constitution.* Madras.

53. John. M. Piphiner. 1962. *Public Administration, Organization.* Prentice Hall, New York.

54. Haridwar Rai and Singh S.P. 1978. *Current Ideas and the Issues in Indian Administration.* Vishal Publications. New Delhi.

55. Harrison Chandra Sharma. 1987. *Public Administration in India.* Jaipur.

56. Hanson, H.A. 1962. *Managerial Problems in Public Enterprises.* Vivek Publications. Delhi.

57. Kaushik S.C. and Pradeep Shahi. (Eds.) 1983. *Public Administration in India, Emerging Trends,* Allahabad.

58. Khanna, R.L.P. 1968. *Public Administration in India,* Chandigarh.

59. Kingsley, Donald, G., *Representative Bureaucracy.* London.

60. Kothari Rajni. 1972. *Politics in India.* Orient Longman Publication, New Delhi.

61. Krisnamachari V.T. 1962. *Report on Indian and State Administrative Service and problems of District Administration,* Planning Commission, Government of India, New Delhi.

62. Kulkarni, P.V. 1981. *Financial Management – A Conceptual Approach,* Oxford. Bombay.

63. Kuchahal. S.C. 1987. *The Industrial Economy of India.* Allahabad.

64. Leman. F. 1976. (Ed.) *The Management of Change in Government.* Hague.

65. Maheshwari Shriram. 1998. *Administrative Theory: An Introduction,* Vishal Publications. New Delhi.

66. ------------- 1998. *Administrative Thinkers.* Macmillan. New Delhi.

67. ------------- 1974. *Indian Administration.* Orient Longman. New Delhi.

68. ------------- 1970. *The Evolution of Indian Administration.* Lakshmi Narayan Agrawal Publications. Agra.

69. Maddick. H. 1970. *Panchayati Raj in India,* Longman, London.

70. Mathur Kuldip. 1972. *Bureaucratic Response to Development: a Study of Block Development Officers in Rajasthan, Uttar Pradesh and Delhi.* New Delhi.

71. Marx, Morstein Friz. (Ed.) 1969. *Elements of Public Administration.* Prentice Hall of India. Pvt. Ltd. New Delhi.

72. Malley. 1965. *The Indian Civil Service.* Princeton, London.

73. Mehta B. 1975. *Dynamics of State Administration,* Allahabad.

74. Maxwell. 1937. *Organization and Procedure,* Maxwell Committee, Delhi.

75. Mathur K. 1972. *Bureaucratic Response,* Vivek, Delhi.

76. Misra B. B. 1983. *District Administration and Rural Development: Policy, Objective and Administrative Change in Historical Perspective,* Oxford University Press, Delhi.

77. ------------- 1947. *The Indian Political Parties: A Historical Analysis of Development up to 1947.* Oxford University Press. Delhi.

78. ------------- 1948. *The Central Administration of the East India Company 1773-1834,* Oxford University Press, Manchester.

79. ------------ 1961. *Indian Middle Class,* Oxford Publication, London.

80. ------------ 1970. *The Administrative History of India — 1834-1947*, Oxford University Press. Bombay.

81. ------------ 1962. *The Bureaucracy in India, a Historical Analysis of Development.* Mittal. Delhi.

82. ------------ 1976. *Government and Bureaucracy in India 1947-76.* Mittal, New Delhi.

83. Mojit Bhattacharya 1991. *Public Administration: Structure, Process and Behaviour,* Oxford University Press, Calcutta.

84. Mukherjee, B.B. 1948. *Administrative Problems of India: Corruption in Public Administration and its Remedies.* Calcutta.

85. Mukherji, P. 1918. *Indian Constitutional Documents*. Calcutta.

86. Narain Luxmi. 1980. *Municipal and Urban India,* Agrawal Publications. New Delhi.

87. Panda Basudev. 1978. *Indian Bureaucracy: An Inside Story,* Mittal, New Delhi.

88. Pai, P. 1966. *Personnel System for Development Administration,* Popular Prakashan, Bombay.

89. Patter. D.C. 1964. *Government in Rural India,* Penguin, London.

90. Prasad. A. D. 1968. *Corruption and Administration,* Basant Publication, Patna.

91. Payelee, M.V. 1967. *Indian Constitution,* Popular Prakashan, Bombay.

92. Paul Appleby. 1953. *Public Administration in India: Report of Survey,* Mittal, New Delhi.

93. Philips, A. T., and Sivaji K. H. 1981. *Indian Government and Politics,* Deep and Deep, New Delhi.

94. Puri, B.N. 1968. *History of Indian Administration,* Vol. I, Popular Prakashan, Bombay.

95. ------------ 1975. *History of Indian Administration* Vol. II, Popular Prakashan, Bombay.

96. Qureshi, A. D. 1979. *The Administrators of Mughal Empire,* New Delhi.

97. Rajneesh, S. 2002. *Rural Development Through Democratic Decentralization,* Deep and Deep Publications, New Delhi.

98. Rai H and S.P. Singh. 1979. *Current Ideal and Issues in Indian Administration.* New Delhi.

99. Rai Mangat E.N. 1976. *Patterns of Administrative Development in Independent India,* University of London.

100. Rao, P.V.R. 1970. *Red Tape and White Cap,* Orient Longman. New Delhi.

101. Ram Jakhar Bal. 1982. *The People, the Parliament and Administration,* New Delhi.

102. Roy. N.C. 1960. *The Civil Service in India,* Jaipal, Calcutta.

103. Rourke Francis. 1976. *Bureaucracy, Politic and Public Policy,* Little Brown, Boston.

104. Spru, R.K. 1977. *Development and Development Administration,* Mahindra Publication, Chandigarh.

105. Sharma, S. K. 1991. *Corruption in Indian Politics and Bureaucracy,* ESS Publications. New Delhi.

106. Sharma, P. 1978. *Public Administration in India.* Meerut.

107. Sharma P.D. 1977. *Indian Police: A Development Approach,* Delhi.

108. Sexena, P.A. 1974. *Training and Development in Government,* Indian Institute of Public Administration, New Delhi.

109. Sharma S.K. & S.L. Malhotra. 1977. *Integrated Rural Development Approach Strategy and Perspectives,* New Delhi.

110. Singh Mohinder. (Ed). 1993. *Some Aspects of Public Enterprises in India: A Plea for Reform,* Deep and Deep, New Delhi.

111. Singh Hoshiar and Singh Mohinder. 1993. *Public Administration in India: Theory and Practice,* Sage Publications, New Delhi.

112. Singh Hoshiar. (ED). 1985. *Rural Development in India,* Jaipur.

113. Singh Hoshiar and Singh D.P. (Eds.) 1990. *Indian Administration: Current Issues and Problems,* Jaipur.

114. Singh Chandrika. 1986. *Socialism in India: Rise, Growth and Prospects.* Mittal Publications, New Delhi.

115. Social Policy and Rural Institutions, Orient Longman, New Delhi.

116. Singh Narendra Kumar. 1974. *Bureaucracy: Position and Persons,* Abinas Publication. New Delhi.

117. Smith, B.C. 1988. *Bureaucracy and Political Power,* Martin's Press, New York.

118. Stahl, O Glenn, 1963. *Public Personnel Administration.* Harper and Row, New York.

119. Subramanian V. 1971. *Social Background of India's Administration: Socio-Economic Study of Higher Civil Service of India,* Publication Division, Ministry of Information and Broadcasting, New Delhi.

120. Singhvi, L.M. 1987. *Parliament and Administration in India,* Deep and Deep, New Delhi.

121. Sinha, V.M. 1987. *Civil Administration and Departments,* Jaipur.

122. Taub Richard, P. 1969. *Bureaucrats under Stress: Administrators and Administration in Indian State,* Burkley University of California Press, California.

123. Thakur, R. 1981. *Elite Theory and Administrative System.* Sterling Publications, New Delhi.

124. Thakur, B.K. 1926. *Indian Administration to the Dawn of Representative Government,* Oxford, Bombay.

125. Torrey William. 1953. *Public Personnel Management, Longman,* New York.

126. Thavara, M.K. 1992. *Financial Administration of India,* New Delhi.

127. Trivedi, K.B. 1987. *Perspective in Development Administration,* Mittal, New Delhi.

128. Tyagi, A.R. 1969. *Civil Services in a Developing Society,* Sterling. New Delhi.

129. Udgaonkar. 1956. *The Political Institution and Administration of Northern India during the Medieval Times,* New Delhi.

130. Verma, R.S. 1973. *Bureaucracy in India,* Progress Publishers, Bhopal.

131. Verma S.P., and Sharma, S.K. 1980. *Managing Public Personnel System: A Comparative Perspective,* Indian Institute of Public Administration, New Delhi.

132. Verma, B. M. and B.P. Singh. 1991. *Integrated Rural Development Programme,* Vivek Publications. New Delhi.

133. Weber Max. 1964. *The Theory of Socio-Economic Organization,* Trans A.H. Henderson, Free Press. New York.

134. Wilenski. Peter. 1968. *Public Power and Public Administration,* Sydney Hale and Ironmonger.

135. White. L.D. 1968. *Introduction to the Study of Public Administration,* Macmillan, New York.

136. Woodhouse Diana. 1997. *In Pursuit of Good Administration, Ministers, Civil Servants and Judges,* Oxford Clarendon Press.

ARTICLES

1. Chandra, M. "Bureaucracy in India since Liberalization", Bhartwal and K. Kishore (Eds.), 2003. Public Administration in India, p. 124.

2. Edward Weinder, "Development Administration: A New Focus of Research approach to Development", in Bhartwal and K. Kishore (Eds.) *Public Administration in India,* op. cit. 259.

3. Dubhasi P.R. 1948. "Leadership role of the Collector", *Indian Journal of Public Administration,* Vol. XI. No. 3.

4. Fazal, M. 1983. "Management Effectiveness in Public Sector", *Lok Yodyog,* Vol. XVIII, No. 1, April.

5. Guha Ramachandra, "Politics and Play", in the *Telegraph,* April 2, 2005.

6. Iqbal Narain, "Administrative challenges to Panchayati Raj", *Indian Journal of Public Administration,* July-September, 1966.

7. Jagnathan, V., "Administration and Citizens", *Indian Journal of Public Administration,* Vol. XII, No. 4, October, December, 1971.

8. Lata Swarn, "Indian Bureaucracy since Liberalization", in Bhartwal and K. Kishore, (Eds.) *Public Administration in India*, op. cit. p. 92.

9. Lajpat Ardent, "The Puzzle of Indian Democracy: A Constitutional Interpretation", *American Political Science Review,* Vol. 90, No. 2, June, 1986. pp. 258-68.

10. Mehta, B., "District Administration in the Past and future", *Indian Journal of Public Administration,* Vol. XVI, No. 3, July-September, 1971.

11. Misra, S.N., "People's Participation in Rural Development Programmes", in Mohindra Singh (1992), (Ed.), Rural Development in India" *Current Perspectives*, New Delhi, p. 126.

12. Misra, S.N. and Verma, B.N., "Evolution of Training of Rural Youth for Self-employment in Rajasthan", *Indian Institute of Public Administration,* New Delhi, 1978.

13. Maithani, B.P., "Organization for Rural Development in North East Region", in P.D. & U. Phukon. 1989. (Eds.) Rural Development North East India, New Delhi, p. 49.

14. Pathak Rahul, "Judiciary Crumbing Citadel", in *India Today,* June 30, 1992.

15. Pandey, J., "Bureaucracy in Bihar: a Surgical Operation on Gandhian Lines", Bhartwal and K. Kishore, (Eds.) *Public Administration in India,* op. cit., pp. 168-75.

16. Parseer, A.P., "Role of Generalist and Specialist in Public Administration", *Indian Journal of Public Administration,* Vol. VVI, April-June, 1975.

17. Presthus Robert, "Decline of the Generalist Myth", *Public Administration Review,* Vol. 24, November-December, 1964.

18. Rabishanker, a, & Jayanthi, b., "Bureaucracy in Public Centre Organizations: Approaches to Improving Competitiveness", Bhartwal and K. Kishore (Eds.) op. cit., p. 168.

19. Reddy G. Ram, "Panchayatiraj Proposals", paper presented in the seminar held at new Delhi, in February 1979.

20. Ropy, T.K., "Some Thoughts on community Participation", *Kurukshetra, vol. XXXI.* May 16-31, 1983, p. 18.

21. Singh, G.P., "Teaching and Research in Public Administration: An Overview", in Bhartwal and K. Kishore (Eds.), *Public Administration in India,* op. cit., p. 40

22. Shiviah, "Decentralization and Panchayati Raj" A Development Perspective", *Indian Journal of Public Administration. XXIV,* July-September, 1978.

23. Saxena, V., "Issues in Development Research" in Bhartwal and K. Kishore (Eds.), *Public Administration in India,* op. cit. p. 79

24. Shastry, C. Sriniwas, "Structure and pattern of Panchayati Raj", *Indian Journal of Public Administration, Vol. VIII,* No. 4, October-November, 1992, p. 460.

25. Singh, P.N., "Rural Development: Some Basic Issues" in Devendra K. Das (Ed.) 1998. *Indian Economy after 50 years of Independence Experience and Challenges,* New Delhi, p. 9.

26. Shakdher, S.L. 1978. "Administrative Accountability to Parliament", *Indian Journal of Public Administration, vol. XII,* No. 3.

27. Satyasen J., "A New Reflection on Participation in the Developed and developing Countries" S.K. Sharma, (1977), (Ed.) *Dynamics of Development Vol. II,* Delhi, p. 110.

28. Singh Radha Raman & Narayan R., "IRDP Revitalization of Rural Scene in India", *Khadi Gramodyog, Vol. XXXX* No. 4, January, 1985, Bombay, p. 177.

29. Singh Charna, "Politician Vs. Civil Servants", *The Illustrated Weekly,* No. 1, 1977.

30. Somjee A.H., "Social Perspective on Corruption in India", *Political Science Review, Vol. 13,* No. 1-4, December-January, 1974.

31. Usha, K., "Challenges of Bureaucracy in India since Independence", Bhartwal and K. Kishore, (Eds.), *Public Administration in India,* op. cit. p. 143.

32. Verma, S.P., "Corruption and Political envelopment in India", *Political; Science Review, Vol. 13,* No. 104, December-January. 1974, p. 172.

33. Whatia. L.M., "Central Vigilance Commission: Its Role in Administrative Vigilance", *Indian Journal of Public Administration Vol. XVII,* No. 1, January, March. 1971.

34. Wheare, K.C., Machinery of Government, *Public Administration, Vol. XXIV,* No. 2, 1946.

REPORTS

1. ARC Interim Report on the Machinery for Planning, Government of India, New Delhi, 1967.
2. Annual Report of the Ministry of Home Affairs, Department of Administrative Reforms, GOI, New Delhi. 1964-65.
3. Famine Commission Report Part-I Para-47-49, New Delhi, 1980.
4. Inamdar, N.R., Report of Study of the Administration of Community Development Block, Haveli University of Poona, 1962, pp. 19-25.
5. Nehru's Message, Summary Record of Annual Conference on Community Development held at Mount Abu, published by the Ministry of Community Development, GOI, New Delhi, 1950, p. 13.
6. Report of the Indian Commission, Part-I, 1980.
7. Report of Indian Constitutional Reforms, 1928.
8. Report of ARC Study Team on Machinery of the Government of India and Procedure of Work, Delhi, 1967. pp. 26-28.
9. Report of the Reorganization of the Machinery of Government, Ayyangar Report, 1949, New Delhi, 1957. Para-14.
10. Report of the Team for the Study of Community Project and National Extension Service, Vol. I, New Delhi, 1956-57, Part-I, Para-2-8. pp 5-7.
11. Report of the Committee on Prevention of Corruption, Para 2-16 and Para 10-11. Ministry of Home Affairs, GOI, New Delhi, 1964,
12. Report of Rural Urban Relationship Committee, GOI, New Delhi, 1966. pp 1-10.

13. Report of Santhanam Committee of India, published by the GOI, New Delhi, March, 1964.

14. Seventh Evaluation Report on Community Development and Allied Fields Programme, Planning Commission of India, New Delhi, 1998.

15. Report of the Team for the Study of Community Project and National Extension Service Vol. I, p. 3.

16. Report of the Study Team on Personnel Administration (Chairman Part, R.K.), August 1967, Delhi, 1969.

17. Report of the Study Team (Machinery of the Government of Indian and its Procedure of Work), Part-I, March, 1967.

18. Report of the Study Team (Machinery of the Government of India and its Procedures of Work Part-II, (Annexure), February, 1968.

19. Report on the Management for Strengthening Administrative Services. Department of Administrative Reforms, Ministry of Home Affairs, GOI, Vol. I and Vol. II, May, 1968.

20. Report of the Royal Commission on Decentralization in India, Vol. I, 1909.

21. Report of the Central Vigilance Commission (annual), first to ninth Report, 1964-65 to 1972-73.

22. Report of the Commission of Inquiry (S.R. Das Commission, 1963), appointed by the GOI to report on the allegations made against Sardar Pratap Singh.

23. Report on the Indian Union Public Service Commission from 1950 to 1973.

24. Planning Commission Report on Indian and State Administrative Services and Problems of District Administration by V.T. Krishnamachari.

JOURNALS, MAGAZINES, WEEKLY, NEWSPAPERS

1. *Indian Journal of Public Administration.*

2. *Indian Journal of Political Science Association.*

3. *American Review of Political Science.*

4. *Journal of the National Academy of Administration*

5. *Political Science Review.*

6. *Kurukshetra.*

7. *Illustrated Weekly.*

8. *Gramin Vikash News letter,* published by the Department of Rural Development, Government of India, New Delhi.

9. *The Hindustan Times,* New Delhi.

10. *The Telegraph,* Calcutta.

11. *The Hindu,* Madras.

12. *The Statesman,* New Delhi and Calcutta.

13. *The Times of India,* New Delhi.

14. *The Nagaland Post,* Dimapur.

15. *The Nagaland Page,* Dimapur.

Index

Administration, 7, 8, 13, 15, 18, 20, 22, 24, 29, 38-41, 44-47, 50, 51, 54-57, 60, 67, 85, 86, 107, 123, 151, 152, 154, 156, 161, 162, 169, 170-174
- Bureaucratic, 20
- Civil, 20
- District, 44-46
- In Ancient India, 40
- Military, 41, 42
- Public, 8, 25, 97, 161
- Rural, 44
- Scope of-, 15
- System, 56
- Technical, 71

Administrative
- Centres, 57
- Changes, 68
- Corruption, 158
- Decision Making, 107
- Ethics, 168-170
- Hierarchal, 9
- Hierarchy of India, 84
- In India, 39, 43, 45, 174
- Infrastructure, 151
- Jobs, 68
- Machinery, 14, 29, 93, 98, 158, 171
- Monolithic, 9
- Reform Committee, 86, 87
- Services, 29, 107
- Structure, 9, 13, 43, 92, 152
- System, 41, 48, 49, 58, 166
- Transformation, 89

Administrators, 53, 93

Afro-Asian Countries, 27

Agricultural
- Development, 100
- Economy, 146
- Labourers, 115
- Methodology, 93
- Operations, 41

Aitcheson Commission, 51

Akbar the Great, 41

All India
- Congress Committee (AICC), 95, 96
- Medical Services, 52
- National Congress, 49
- Services, 47, 51, 71, 81, 82
- Service Amendment Act, 1963, 9

Act, 82

Amendment Act, 82

Alleviate Poverty, 65, 88, 112, 118

Altruism, 7

Amatyas (ministers), 40

Ambedkar, BR, 161

American Funding Agencies, 25
Ancient
  Administrative Pattern of India, 40
  Panchayat System, 60
Anti-Corruption Drive, 121
Anti-Poverty Programme, 115, 125
Area Planning Schemes, 129
Article-Indian Constitution,
  315(1), 76
    124, 148, 218, 320, 73
    14, 15, 16, 29-20, 80
  309, 81
  310(2), 72
  311, 72, 74
  312(2), 72, 74
  312, 82
  316, 76, 77
  323(1), 80
Asia and Africa, Democracies of-, 29
Asok Mehta Committee, 110
Award of Pension, 79
Ayyanger, N, Gopalaswami, 84, 86

Backward Classes, 87, 171
Backwardness to Forwardness, 13
Balvantrai Mehta Committee Report, 101, 105
Banking, 31
Basu, DD, 80, 82
Below Poverty Line (BPL), 14, 43, 108, 113, 114, 117, 119, 128, 132, 134
Bhagawati, PN, Chief Justice, 163
Bhartiya Janata Party (BJP), 118
Blau, Peter, 8, 18
Block
  Budget Formulation, 104
  Development, 154
  Development Officer (BDO), 99, 103, 104, 106, 111, 122
  Samiti, 102, 103
  System of American Type, 109
Board of Revenues, 46
British
  Administration, 57
  Administration in India, 50
  Administration System, 38-63
  Administrators, 59, 60
  Bureaucracy, 152
  Bureaucratic Pattern, 66
  Bureaucratic System, 39
  Bureaucrats, 56, 60
  Cabinet in England, 48
  Civil Servants, 56
  Colonial Rule, 70
  Crown's Government, 43
  Democratic and Administrative Model, 39
  Developed Towns, 39
  Madras, 39
  Shillong, Kanpur, Surat, 39
  Bombay, 39
  Calcutta, 39
  Delhi, Guwahati, 39
  Economic Policy, 94
  Empire, 49
  Government in India, 47
  India, 50, 51
  India and Legacy, 38-63
  India Government, 43, 48, 64

Model of Bureaucracy, 70
Model of Civil Service Commission, 75
Parliament, 48
Parliament in England, 44
Pattern of Bureaucratic Administration, 21
Raj, 39
Regime, 39, 46, 60, 103, 155
Regime in India, 30
Rule, 39, 43, 53-55, 151, 171
Rule in India, 9, 48, 94
Rulers, 55, 58, 59
Rulers and Administrative System un India, 43
Stooges, 60
Style of Administration, 99
System, 21, 57
System of Administration, 71
Broad Based Training System, 132
Brokers, 174
Bureaucracy, 7, 8, 13-37, 53-55, 68, 92-123, 151-178
American Idea of-, 17
And Civil Service, 20
And Rural Development, 13-37
Changes in-, 92
Defined, 15, 16
Despotic, 8
In India, 9, 46
In Western View, 16, 17
Instrumental View, 18
Modern, 19
Nature of-, 18
Organizational Pattern of-, 14
Organizational Structure, 152
Role of-, 7, 19
Scope, 15
Bureaucratic
Administration, 17, 20
In India, 44
Administrative System, 7
Changes in-, 64-89
Despotism, 66
Development, 17
Dominance in Community Development Programme, 100
Framework, 64-89
Interference, 102
Intervention, 104
Model in India, 21, 83
System, 14
And Political Corruption-Nexus, 159-160
Bureaucratism, Democratism, and Decentralization, 105
Bureaucratization, 106
Bureaucrats, 7, 8, 11, 16, 19, 30, 31, 53, 54, 151-154, 160, 163, 165, 167, 169-171, 175, 176
Role of-, 11
Business Management, 18

Cabinet Secretariat, 83, 84
Basic Performance, 86
Cadre of Civil Services,
Reservations in-, 54, 55
Capitalism, 18, 23, 28
Capitalist Society in India, 64

Capitalistic
Pattern to Socialistic Pattern, 96
Capitalistic System,
Abolution of, 28
Carpentry—Soldering, 122
Cash Employment Program, 112
Caste and Religious Politics, 170
Central
Assistance, 116
Board of Irrigation and Power, 153
Bureau of Investigation (CBI), 165
Employment Guarantee Council, 147
Services, 81
Statistical Organization, 84
System, 28
Vigilance Commission, 165
Centralization, 105
Of Administration, 57
Centrally Sponsored Schemes, 128-148
Achievements and Failures, 128-148
Centres of Administration and Business, 39
Madras—Surat, 39
Chandragupta, 40
Uniform Pattern of Administration, 40
Charter Act, 1833, 44, 47
Chelmsford, Montague, 49
Chief Election Commissioner, 73
Chinese Aggression 1962, 155
Civil Servants, 71-73
Constitutional Protection to-, 71
Civil Services, 20, 21, 44, 51, 52, 54, 67-70, 75, 78, 79, 161, 171
In Great Britain, 29
Class War, 16
Coinage, 31
Collection of
Public Revenues, 45
Revenues and Punishment, 41
Colonial
Administrative Pattern, 43
Masters, 59
Period, 169
Power, 70
Rule, 8, 29
Commercial
Banks, 112
Business, 46
Committee on
Plan Projects, 10, 97
Prevention of Corruption, 156, 162
Communal Representation, 55
Communications, 31
Communist Party, 62
Of India, 96
Community Development, 98
Administration, 103
Blocks, 104
Programme, (CDP), 32, 33, 97-102, 104105, 109, 121, 154, 157
Objectives, 99
Projects (CDP), 1952, 10
Company's Trade in 1833, 45
Compulsory Retirement, 74
Congress
Committee of Uttar Pradesh, 95
Government under Nehru, 108
Leaders, 96

Consolidated Fund of India, 79
Constituent Assembly, 68, 69
Constitution of India, 9, 31, 32, 66, 68, 73, 75
Constitutional
  Power, 81
  Protection, 28
Copland, Sir Reginald, 49
Corporate Group, 19
Corruption, 70, 137, 156-164
  Among Bureaucrats, 155-158
  And Criminalization on Public Life, 162
  And Mismanagement of Funds, 89
  In India, 155, 162
  In Indian Administrative System, 156
  Rise of-, 168
Cottage Industries, 113
Council
  For Advancement of People's Action and Rural Technology, 135
  Of State, 49
Credit Facilities on Cheap Rate, 134
Credit-cum-Subsidy Program, 143, 144
  Analysis, 144
  Currency, 31

Dahl, Robert, 38
Daily Employment Allowance, 146
Dairy
  Development, 135
  Farms, 29
Dairy and Running of Small Shops, etc. 114
Dandekar and Nilakantha, 122
Dantewala Committee, 111
Decentralization of Power, 31, 101, 103, 110, 154, 176
Decentralized Sector, 135
Deforestation and Soil Erosion, 146
Delhi Police Establishment, 164
Demand for Reservations, 56
Democracy and
  Industrialization, 14
  Socialism, 26
Democratic
  Decentralization, 102
  Socialism, 14, 17
Desai, AR, 95
Despotism, 29
Development
  Administration, 7-12, 13-15, 19, 22, 23, 24, 26, 27, 29, 31, 32, 33, 59, 60, 65, 89, 92, 93, 98, 101107, 111, 158, 160, 162, 166, 167, 174, 176
  And Social Change, 88
  And Socio-Economic Justice, 27
  Basic Objectives, 9, 26
  Concept of-, 29
  Conceptual Meaning of-, 21
  Defined, 9
  Growth of-, 25
  In India, 11, 151-153
  Plans, 112
  Planning, 9
  Policy Making, 9
  Process of-, 13
  Programmes, 9
  Projects, 9

Plans and Programs, 14
Policies and Programs, 15
Programme, 60, 92, 106, 107, 109, 113, 155
Schemes, 29
Schemes and Programs, 14, 92
Schemes and Projects, 9
Diarchy, 53
Dihs, 42
Directive Principles of State Policy, 66, 89
Disciplinary Matters, 79
District
Administration, 44-46
Collectors, 104
Industries Centres (DIC), 115, 116, 129
Rural Development Agency (DRDA), 114, 128, 133, 142, 143
Division of Work, 18
Drought Prone Area Program (DPAP), 112, 118, 129
DWCRA (Development of Women and Children in Rural Areas), 142

East India Company, 20, 21, 43, 44, 46-48, 70
Corrupt, 44
Government, 43
Economic
Administration, 86
And Social Justice, 93
And Social Structure, 95
Backwardness, 8
Development, 43, 108, 128, 151, 161
Development Program, 98
Policy (ies), 94, 96, 97
Power, 108
Structure of Society, 95
System of Parasitic—Stagnation, 94
Economy, 29, 132
Agricultural, 146
Indian, 10
Mixed, 30
Of India, 8
Education, 113
Educational Institutions, 20
Election Campaign, 112
Electorates, 170
Employment Guarantee, 136
English Bureaucrats, 53
Environmental Protection, 9, 26
Eradicate (Eradication) Poverty, 10, 64, 119, 129, 135, 174
Ethics, 169
Exchequer and Revenue under Wazirs or Diwans, 42
Executive and Judicial Powers, 41

Family Planning, 113
Federal
Public Service Commission, 75
Service Commission, 56
Financial
And Technical Assistance, 137
Institutions, (FIs), 31
Resources, 100
First
Congress Government, 9
World War Outbreak, 52

Five Year Plan
(2nd), 108, 164
(3rd), 104
(6th), 10, 115, 131
(7th), 10, 115, 131, 136
Five Year Plans, 9, 97, 100, 101, 128
Fodder Production, 135
Food
For Work, (FFW), 118, 120
Stamps, 24
Foreign Technology, 46
Formalism, 16
Fortification, 41
Freedom
Movement, 56, 94-96
Struggle, 96, 97, 153
Fundamental Rights, 80, 81, 96

Gandhi, Mahatma, 61, 96
Philosophy of-, 62
Gandhi, Mrs. Indira, PM, 10, 88, 111, 112, 128, 133, 167
Gandhi, Rajiv, former PM, 10, 117, 133, 137
Garibi Hatao, 177
Geological and Archaeological Survey of India, 51
Golden Jubilee Rural Housing Scheme, 144
Good Governance, 8, 9, 22, 26, 39, 111
Government of India Acts 1861, 1892, 1909, 48
Act 1858, 47
Act 1919, 49, 50
Act 1935, 46, 75, 76
Governor General
Council, 47
In Council, 54, 44
Of Bengal, 44, 47
Gram
Panchayat, 146, 147
Sabha, 143
Sevak, 101, 103, 106, 177
Great Britain, 60
see also British
Grievances Redressal Mechanism, 147
Grow More Food Enquiry Committee, 98
Guaranteed Wage Employment, 145

HADP, 118, 120
Harijans, 96
And Adivasis, 122
Haveli Block Advisory Committee, 104
Health Education, 29
Hierarchal Line of Control, 8
Hierarchy, 18
Hindus and Muslims, 155
Divide, 55
Honey Keeping, 114
Human Development Report, 23

IAY (Indira Awas Yojna), 117, 118, 130, 142-144, 178
Ideologies
And Principles, 32, 161
Of Socialism, 173
Ideology of Individualism, 28
Imperialism, 65

Income Distribution, 94
India, A Capitalist State, 109
India's
  Administrative and Business Creation Framework, 39
  Federal System, 50
  Freedom, 96
  Independence, 1947, 38, 96, 122
Indian
  Administration, 46, 51, 54, 58, 153
  Administrative System (IAS), 11, 39, 43, 46, 48, 50, 55, 71, 72, 81, 83, 87, 88, 89, 155, 164, 167, 174
  Administrators, 9, 54, 151
  Administrators and Bureaucrats, 69
  Agricultural Services, 51, 82
  Audit and Accounts Service, 81
  Bureaucracy, 43, 53, 54, 55, 151
  Bureaucratic System, 9
  Structural, Functional Base—, 9
  Bureaucrats, 88, 153-155, 158, 159
  Civil Service (ICS), 47, 55, 56, 64, 69, 71, 153
  Commercial Houses, 163
  Constitution, 67-71, 88, 93
  Constitutional Assembly, 59
  Courts, 105
  Custom and Excise Services, 81
  Economic Services, 82
  Economy, 10
  Education Services, 51, 82
  Electorate, 88
  Engineering Services, 82
  Federal System, 155
  Foreign Services, 81
  Forest Services, 51, 82
  Intellectuals, 51
  Leaders, 56, 96
  Legislatures, 55
  Medical Services, 51, 82
  Muslims, 55, 56
  National Congress, (INC), 62, 95, 96, 97, 119, 152
  Parliament, 82
  Planning Commission, 156, 173
  Planning, 88
  Police, 51
  Police Service (IPS), 71, 71, 81, 83, 167, 174
  Political and Administrative System, 38
  Political Leaders, 51
  Revenues, 48
  Services of Engineers (Created in 1892), 51
  Society, 96
  Traditions and Conventions, 39
  Veterinary Services, 51
Individualism, 64
Industrial
  Development, 134, 154
  Policy (1948), 30
  Policy Resolution, 164
Industrialization, 7, 14, 27, 35, 162
  Growth of-, 7
  Rise of-, 18
Industries, 134, 135
  Domestic, 43
  Village and Small Scale-, 98
Industry Service Business (ISB), 129, 133
Inefficiency and Red Tape, 14

Infrastructure, 118, 121, 153
And Marketing, 142
Facilities, 113, 114
Institutional Development, 9, 26
Integrated Rural Development Programme (IRDP), 10, 33, 112-116, 120, 121, 129, 130, 132, 135, 137, 141, 142
Components, 115
ISB (Industry Service and Business), 115
Components, TRYSEM, 115
Intensive Agricultural Area Programme, (IAAP), 112
Iron and Steel Ministry, 165
Irrigation, 46
Project Area Program, (IPAP), 112
Irrigational Planning, 93
Issue of Kashmir, 155

Jawahar Rozgar Yojana (JRY), 116-118, 121, 130, 137-142, 178
General Services, 141
Works under—, 139, 140
Jeevan Nair and UC Jain, 29, 30
JGSY (Jawahar Gram Samridhi Yojana), 118, 142
Job Card, 146, 148
Joint State Public Service Commission, 76
Judicial
Activism, 166
Administration, 50
System, 163
Judiciary, 161
Justice—Public Morality, 66

Karachi Sessions, 95
Karl Marx, 16
Kashmir, 155
Kautilya's Arthashastra, 40
Khadi and Village Industry Corporation, 116
Khan-i-Samen or High Steward, 42
Khera, Sujan Singh, Secy Cabinet Sectt, 87
Knowledge and Tectonics of Birth Control, 137

Labour Union, 96
Lahore and Karachi Sessions, 95
Laissezfaire Economic Order, 32
Lajpat Rai, 95
Land Reforms Measures, 113
Landless Labourers, 100
Landlordism, 39
Law and Order, 8, 15, 22, 29, 41, 45, 171
Laws and Regulations, 47
Leadership in India, 39
Legacy of British Rule, 70
In Indian Administration, 70
Legal and Judicial System, 57
Legislation, 28
Legislative
Assembly, 49
Council of Governor General, 44
Leviathan, 23
Liberalism, 16
Philosophy, 16
Liberalization, Privatization and Globalization (LPG), 31
Litigation, 112

Loan Based Rural Housing Scheme of HUDCO, 144
Loans to Farmers, 98
Local
  Administration, 106, 107
  Development Planning, 102
  Self Government, (LSG), 13, 14
Lord Bentinck, 45
Lord Cornwallis, 57

Macaulay Committee, 70
Maladjustment of Funds, 145
Maladministration, 158
Malpractices, 145
  And Corruption, 176
Manmohan Singh, PM, 119
Marketing Outlets, 135
Marxism, 22, 26
Marxist Thought, 27
Mass Corruption, 11
Maternity Benefits, 28
Max Weber, 15-17, 19
Medieval India, 41
Mehta
  Committee, 101, 102, 103, 104, 106, 110
  Study Team, 105, 107
MFAL Programme, 118, 120
Micro Enterprises in Rural Areas, 118
Migration of Labourers, 119
Military
  Administration, 41, 42
  Pay and Accounts Officer, 42
Mill, John Stuart, 38
Million Wells Scheme (MWS), 130, 142
Minimum Need Program, 112
Ministers and Bureaucrats, 170
Ministries and Bureaucrats, 67
Ministry of
  Home Affairs, 165
  Rural Development, 144
  Minor Irrigation, 135
Minority
  Community, 55
  Groups, 55
Mir-i-Baksh, 42
Mixed Economy, 30
Modern
  Techniques and Facilities, 144
  Technology, 110
Modernization, 162
  Of Farming, 94
Monarchy, 21, 40
Moneymaking Pursuits, 174
Monolithic—Hierarchal Administrative System, 39
Montgomery, 25
Moral Standards, 159, 161, 169, 175
  In Public Life, 11
Morality, 158, 159, 162, 168
Morstein, 15
Movement of Communism, 22
Mrs. Gandhi's Government, 112 *see also under* Gandhi, Mrs. Indira
Mughal
  Administrative System, 43
  Empire, 41, 42
  Rulers, 42, 44
Muir, Ramsay, 29

Mukhyas, 177
Multi-Ethnic Societies, 38

Nation Building, 101
National
  Democratic Alliance (NDA), 118, 141
  Development Council, (NDC), 10, 97, 105, 173
    Conference, 115
  Extension Service (NES), 97, 99-101, 157
  Housing Bank, 144
  Monarchy, 21
  Rural Employment Program, (NREP), 116, 117
  Security, 31
Natural Calamities, 64, 65
Nehru, Pandit Jawaharlal, 9, 65, 95, 99, 108, 109, 153-155
  Insistence on Village Development, 98
  Rule, 154
  Style of Administration, 155
  Till Indira Gandhi, 109
Nepotism and Favouritism, 41, 53, 158
Neutral Agency, (Public Service Commission), 8
Neutralism of Bureaucracy, 14
New Social Order, 26
Nexus among Politicians, Criminals, Bureaucrats, 162
NGO, 166
Non-Agricultural Sector, 132
NREGP (National Rural Employment Guarantee Program), 11, 119, 136
NREGS (National Rural Employment Guarantee Scheme), 145-147, 147
  Act, 145-148
NREP (National Rural Employment Program), 10, 135, 137, 138

Old Age Pension, 28
Organization and Management (O&M), 84

Panchayat
  Mandal, 110
  Samitis, 143
Panchayati
  Cell, 106
  Raj, 110, 166
  Raj Act, 109
  Raj Bodies, 105
  Raj Institutions (PRIs), 31, 33, 97, 102, 104, 107, 108, 110, 111, 121, 176
  Raj Phase, 98
  Raj Programmes, 141
  Raj System, 32, 106, 107
Panchayats, 140
Paraganas, 42
Parliamentary
  Democracy, 38, 53
  Government Policies, 30, 31
  System in India, 44, 49
  System, 53
Participation of People in Decision Making, 107, 108

Partition of India,. 155
Party
Politics, 8, 20, 67, 88
System, 14
Peasants Union, 96
Pension Concessions, 24
Reduction, 26
Removal, 94
Schemes, 24
Pension Expenditure, 23
Planned
Economic Development, 32
Model of Development, 32
Planners, 10, 111
Planning, 7, 65, 92, 97, 102, 105, 108, 110, 112, 123, 133, 143
And Policies, 64
And Programs, 86
And Schemes—People's Development, 92
Cell, 111
Centralized, 152
Commission of India, 10, 32, 88, 97, 98, 112, 114, 121, 128, 173
For Rural Development, 111
Plans and
Programmes, 22
Plato, 26
Schemes, 119
Pluralism in Society, 166
PMRY, 131
Policies and Programs, 7, 10, 14, 20, 65, 88, 97, 178
Planning and Objective Projects, 64
Policy
Formation and Implementation, 107
Of Reservation, 56
Of Roosevelt, 27
New Deal, 27
New Freedom, 27
Political
And Administrative System, 42
Bodies, 40
Samiti and Sabha, 40
Democracy, 32
Institutions, 23
Party (ies), 67, 111, 118
Philosophies, 16
Politics and Administration, 55
Politization of Administration, 172
Poverty Alleviation Programme, 9, 26, 107, 112, 113, 137, 177
Schemes, 177
System, 13
And Exploitation, 96
And Illiteracy, 38
Pradhans, 177
Preamble of Constitution, 66, 89
Presidencies of Bombay and Madras, 43
Presidency Governments, 47
Pressure Groups, 163
Indian Chamber of Commerce, 163
State Chamber of Commerce, 163
Trade Association, 163
Prevention of Corruption Act, 157
Prime Minister's Yojana Integrated Urban Poverty, 131
Prime Ministers' Office, 83, 84
Princely India under 562 Princes, 50
Principles of Equality and Liberty, 13

Private
  Ownership, 27
Property, 27
Production and Distribution of Goods, 28
Programme
  Evaluation Organization, 97
  On TRYSEM, 131
Progressive Policies and Programs, 7
Protection to Civil Servants, 80
Provincial
  Civil Services, 56, 57
  Educational Services, 52
Public
  Administration, 25, 97, 161, 164, 166, 169
  Administrative Services, 20
  Finance, 17
  Revenue, 17
  Sector, 31
  Utility Rebates, 24
Public Service Commission (PSC), 8, 44, 54, 69, 71, 75, 76, 87, 158
  Members,
    Functions, 78-80
    Items to be Consulted, 75
    Qualifications and Experience, 76
    Tenure, 76
Purses, 112

Recruiting Agency, 75
Races and Languages, 38
Railway Communication in India, 46
Rajya Sabha (Council of States), 82
Ravishankar and Jayanthi, 166
Recruitment
  For Civil Services in India, 54
  Of Civil Servants, 57
  System in India, 51
  To Public Offices, 158
Recruits of Reservation/Quota, 171
Red and Green Cards, 119
Regulating Act of 1873, 43
Regulations and Acts, 43
Relief
  To Disabled, 28
  Works, 65
Religious Scriptures, 40
Research Program Committee, 10
Reservation (s), 55
  In Jobs and Academic Institutions, 171
  Of Seats, 28, 54, 55
Revenues, 8
Reversion, 74
Revolts by Provincial Rulers, 42
Right to Information, 166
RIP (Rural Industries Program), 129
RLEGP (Rural Landless Employment Guarantee Program), 136-138
RLEP, (Rural Landless Employment Program), 10
Roman Empire, 17
Royal Indian Engineering College, 52
Rural
  Administration, 44, 98, 110, 176
  Artisans Program, (RAP), 115, 129
  Community, 35

Cooperatives, 113
Development, 32, 34, 35, 62, 98, 100, 102, 109, 110, 113118, 120, 121, 133, 154
Defined, 33
In India, 12
Policies and Programs for-, 92
Programme, 101, 114, 117, 118, 119, 145, 174, 176
By NDA Govt., 141
Indira Awas Yojana, 174
Old Age Pension, 174
Schemes, 10, 118, 120
And Program, 128
Schemes of Loans, 174
Economic Face, 114
India, 14, 39, 60, 93, 133, 174
Industries, 129, 132
Industry Program, 115
Labourers Employment Program, 33
Landless, 116
Landless Employment Program (RLEP), 116, 117
Leaders, 135
Planning, 103
Reconstruction, 135
Skilled Workers, 148
Society, 144
Transformation, 35
Workers, 94, 141, 148
Youth Training, 115

Safety of Civil Services, 68
SALA Model of Riggs, 22
Santhanam, K, 156
Committee, 158, 163-165
Sarkar Committee, 165
Sarkars, 42
SAY (Samagra Awas Yojana), 118, 144
Scheduled Castes/Tribes (SC/ST), 33, 56, 87, 102. 115, 121, 136, 143, 145, 171
Women, 118
Schemes and Programs for Village Development, 107
Scientific Administrative System, 44
Second World War, 53, 159
Sector, Public, 31
Self-Development, 35
Programme, 97
Self-Employment, 133, 142
Schemes, 135
Self-Help
Groups (SHGs), 142, 143
Programme, 99
Sericulture, 135
Service Rules, 57
SFDA Programme, 118, 120
SGSY (Swaranjayanti Gram Swarozgar Yojana), 118, 141-143, 178
Shahjahan, 41
Shastri, Lal Bahadur, 109
Shift in Planning, 111
Sickness Benefits, 23
Singh, PN, 94
Sino-Indian Conflict 1962, 108, 109
SITRA, 142

Skilled/Semi-Skilled Workers, 146
  Wages of-, 146
Skills and Trade, 132
  Tailoring, Electrical Fittings—Cycle Repairing, 132
Small
  And Marginal Farmers, 115
  And Marginal Farmers Development Programmes, (SMFDP), 33
  And Tiny Industries, 129
  Industries, 29
  Shops, 114
  Scale Cottage and Tiny Industries, 116
Social
  And Political Justice, 27
  Change, 18
  Classes, 16
  Groups, 18
  Justice, 55
  Order, 69
  Organization, 17
  Pattern of Society, 19
  Reformers, 22
  Reforms, 34
  Safety, 146
  Security Expenditure, 23
  Security Measures, 28
Socialism, 9, 14, 16, 22
  Ideologies, 23
Socialist
  Congress, 96
  Leaders, 96
  Party, 62
  Philosophy, 152
  Principles, 88, 92
Socialistic
  Pattern of Society (SPS) of India, 10, 65, 88, 108
  Principles, 15
Society, 8, 13, 16, 21, 35, 38, 41, 66, 89, 161
  Capitalist (Capitalistic), 8, 22
  Democratic, 13
  Egalitarian, 7, 108
  Indian, 96
  Modern, 14, 18
  Rural, 35, 121, 144
Socialists, 8
Socio-Economic
  Bureaucratic Constraints-, 151-178
  Change, 65
  Development, 38
  Injustice, 27
  Justice, 23, 24, 26-28, 64
  Policies, 64-89
  Transformation, 22
State
  Administration of Rural Development, 104
  Employment Guarantee Council, 147
  Public Service Commission, 78
Structural
  Administrative Organization, 41
  And Institutional Development, 26
  Development, 9
  Mechanism, 110
Structures of Civil Society, 14

Subas, 42
Subedars, 42
Subsidies, 134
Sugar Lobby, 109
Suppression and Exploitation, 61
  Regeneration and Liberation
    from-, 62
Supreme Court
  Judges, 73
  Of India, 74
Swarozgaris, 118, 143
System of
  Administration, 65
  Landlordism, 93
  Recruitment, 45

Technical
  Administration, 71
  Skills, 134
Territorial Welfare, 41
Three Tier Panchayati Raj System, 102, 106
Town and Commercialization, 42
Trade Union, 96
Training Infrastructure, 133
Transfer of Power, 66
TRYSEM (Training Rural Youth for Self-Employment), 10, 129-133, 142
Twenty-Point Programme, 115

Under Privileged, 24
Unemployment, 28
Union Commission, 76, 77, 80
Union Public Service Commission (UPSC), 47, 78, 83, 87
United Nations, 23
  Development Program, 23
United Sates of America, 17, 21, 24, 27
  Bureaucracy, 21
  Bureaucrats, 21
Untouchability, 60

Vajpayee, Atal Behari, PM, 118, 141, 166
Values, Neutral Theory, 8
Vedic Pattern, 40
Village
  Administration, 41, 102
  And Small Scale Industries, 98
  Community, 94
  Industries, 135
  Level Worker (VLW), 106
  Panchayats, 14, 60, 100, 102-104, 117, 146, 147
  Smallest Unit of Administration, 41
  Swaraj, 62
Vocational Training, 122
Voluntary Agencies, 111

Weaker
  And Downtrodden Sections, 93
  Sections, 32, 35
Weber's Concept of Bureaucracy, 18
Weberian
  Formulation, 20
  Ideal Type, 16
Welfare
  Administration, 19

Policies, 23
Schemes, 27
And Programs, 15
State, 8, 9, 14, 23, 28, 32, 68, 92, 169
Defined, 24-25
Western Liberal Thinkers, 16
Winder, 25
Working Class, 22
Rights and Status, 22
World Population, 23

Zamindari, 39
Zamindars, 45
Zilla Parishad, 102-105, 110, 111, 142

NOTES

NOTES